Blame it on the Vicar

Holy Appropriate Tales of Old Somerset

ROGER EVANS

HALSGROVE

British Library Cataloguing-in-Publication Data
A CIP record for this title is available from the British Library

ISBN 1 84114 568 8
ISBN 978 1 84114 568 6

HALSGROVE

Halsgrove House
Lower Moor Way
Tiverton, Devon EX16 6SS
Tel: 01884 243242
Fax: 01884 243325
email: sales@halsgrove.com
website: www.halsgrove.com

Printed and bound by
Antony Rowe Ltd, Chippenham, Wiltshire

Contents

Introduction

Little did I expect to find a scandal involving a vicar so close to home when I embarked on this book, but lo and behold, almost on my doorstep, I discovered a report of a vicar of the parish of Wembdon who, having produced five illegitimate children by women of five different parishes, was caught in bed with mistress number seven whilst number six was close to her confinement in Taunton! Three miles in the other direction, I discovered the Bawdrip-born bishop who was hanged in Dublin gaol, falsely accused of sodomy.

Cast the net slightly further afield and we have mediaeval nuns and monks doing what comes naturally, parsons watering down the communion wine and then turning up drunk, and a house where once the children's programmes of *Camberwick Green* and *Trumpton* were produced turning out to be the centre of a nineteenth-century religious sex cult.

Can it get any worse? Yes, by casting the net to cover the whole county of Somerset, we discover hunting parsons by the score, priests who plotted against the king, vicars who turned detective and those who were so boring that they employed bell ringers to keep the congregation awake.

But it's not all bad news. In this sequel to *Blame it on the Cider*, I also pay credit to those members of the clergy who left as their legacy a lighthouse, a school, *Rock of Ages* and the table fork! Villainous vicars, parsimonious parsons, misbehaving monks, riotous rectors and precocious priests all contribute to this rich collection of holy appropriate tales of old Somerset.

Roger Evans
October 2006

1

Modern Misdemeanours and Medieval Mischief

Modern day phenomenon?

If for whatever reason, you are under the impression that recent sex scandals involving the clergy are a new phenomenon, then read on and we will discover that it has always been that way. We will even go back to the thirteenth century when a prior was satisfying his carnal desire with the local nuns. And then there was the case in 1369 of Robert Thoryng, the parish priest of Stoke Pero who abducted the wife of one of his parishioners. But perhaps a few recent reminders may help to pave the way.

Within the last few years a thirty-nine-year-old Catholic monk from Downside Abbey admitted numerous cases of making indecent photographs of children. An assistant priest at Nailsea's Holy Trinity church was disqualified after admitting an affair with a married woman. A choirmaster from North Somerset was jailed for sexually assaulting a boy with six counts of making indecent photos.

A Devon vicar recently left his wife and family, having resigned his position to live in Somerset with the wife of a bishop. Nowadays, marital problems barely raise an eye-brow. Living as couples outside of marriage is almost becoming the norm. It is paedophilia which makes the headlines rather than clandestine affairs. The modern-day punishment for leaving one's spouse and moving in with someone else's appears to be no greater than the financial burden of a divorce settlement. But it wasn't always that simple. Let's step back in time and consider the harsh penalties of centuries past. Let's begin by considering the case of poor Maude de Merriet.

Maude de Merriet and other naughty nuns

Maude was a thirteenth-century nun at the nunnery in Cannington. Born at Hestercombe, she married a Combe Florey gentleman but embarked on a change of vocation when she became a nun and joined the Benedictine sisters at Cannington. Legend has it that Maude, and two other nuns, stood accused of fraternising with the menfolk of the village, behaviour totally inappropriate for a nun. Their punishment was to be beaten and stoned. Unfortunately it all went badly wrong for Maude who died from the injuries. Too late, her accusers reconsidered the severity of the punishment, concluding that her heart had always been pure. It was only her flesh which was weak. And so they removed her heart, which was buried in the north wall of the church at Combe Florey. An engraved plaque marks the spot. The rest of her mortal remains were buried outside of the church wall in Cannington, in a spot where a modern extension to the *Blue Anchor Inn* was built over her grave. It is her ghost which now haunts that pub, earning it a change of title to the *Friendly Spirit*.

Other nuns also practised inappropriate behaviour. One called Tremlett was found to be 'with child and not by the Holy Ghost.' It was suggested that she was 'frequenting the premises of the prior more than was appropriate for his or her calling.' This again was in the thirteenth century at a time when a church commission was set up to investigate the rumour that nuns were sleeping together. The rumours proved to be well founded.

It seems that the nuns of Barrow Gurney were not much better. At the site of what is now Barrow Court there once stood the Benedictine nunnery of Barrow Mynchin. Just like the Cannington nunnery, it was on the small side, perhaps a dozen or so nuns. Being small, it was probably under-funded and perhaps therein lay the root cause of the lack of discipline. It proved to be a continuous headache for the Bishop of Bath and Wells who wrote to the prioress threatening her with excommunication if she failed to change her unbecoming ways. The nuns under her wing were providing ample evidence that their vows of chastity were not being upheld. They would tart themselves up and then disappear overnight, returning the following morning.

Unable to persuade the prioress to change their practices, the bishop took the unusual step of putting a man in charge and a year later appointed a new prioress, Joan de Gournay. But the bishop had failed to realise that she hadn't even taken her vows and that she would turn out to be worse than the one he had recently dismissed. She actually resigned before the bishop had chance to sack her. Soon after, the bishop gave it up as a bad job and resigned himself.

The venturesome vicars of Wells

The Vicars Close at Wells

Meanwhile, the bishop was also having trouble controlling his Vicars Choral at Wells, a choir consisting of vicars. A wonderful example of our architectural heritage exists at Vicars Close in the city. It was built by the bishop in the hope that by keeping his vicars in one enclosed area, he could keep them from the temptations of the city, in particular the carnal ones. But the ladies who made a living from such liaisons were one step ahead. They would enter the church when the Vicars Choral were performing, on the supposed pretext of selling various wares. However, they only fulfilled their transactions behind the cover of the huge pillars in the cathedral, out of sight of the bishop and the congregation. Various vicars would take it in turns to leave the choir during this period and would return to their places complete with a warm glow! There was little doubt as to what was really going on and in 1298 the bishop issued instructions that all forms of trading within the church were banned and that no vicar was allowed to leave the choir until the service was completely over.

Forty years later and little had changed, except it appears that the vicars were now taking more care with their appearance in order to attract the ladies, and in addition, they were galloping their way through both the hymns and the sermon in order to increase their leisure time at the end of the service. The bishop had to issue further instructions declaring that vicars must wear more suitable clothes, not too long and not too short. The crown of the head had to be shaved and what hair remained was not to cover the ears, as a sign that they had cast aside earthly desires.

The bishop also criticised the amount of time they spent on hunting, fowling, fishing, dancing and masquerading, and prowling the streets singing and shouting and generally having what appeared to be a jolly good time! They would spend long evenings in the ale houses, holding competitions, drinking pint for pint, to see who could best out-drink the others. It sounded very much like belonging to a rugby or carnival club. And they were committing adultery with married women. Perhaps it was to protect themselves from irate husbands that they even carried swords, a practice which was against both civil and clerical law.

2

Sex Scandals of the Seventeenth Century

For centuries, the moralist attitudes of the Church had determined what was or was not acceptable in respect of sexual and marital behaviour. Perhaps this was never more so than in the Puritan days of the early seventeenth century, The Church had determined that the sexual act should only be normal intercourse between husband and wife, and even dictated how and when it was acceptable. The act should be in the 'missionary position', i.e. the woman on her back, and should not take place on holy days when the sacrament was received, nor during Lent. Pre-marital or extra-marital sex was completely taboo and it was not unknown for the local parson to check on couples, even married couples, creeping up to their houses and peering through cracks around the door to check on their behaviour!

People power

During the seventeenth century, there were, however, effectively three "courts" as far as sexual wrong-doing was concerned. There was the Church's ecclesiastical court, the state court and the 'people's court'. The latter had no official standing but was perhaps the most feared. The problem came from the fact that an illegitimate child and its mother, if no father owned up to paternity, became the financial responsibility of the parish. Overwhelmingly country folk struggled to survive without having to support other people's offspring. Hence the unmarried mother was shunned and shamed, and often disgraced sufficiently to drive her out of the community from where she would take to the open road, driven from parish to parish until the child was born. The normal procedure was for the people of the village to sort the problem out themselves. If that failed, they complained to the clergy, and if they failed, they escalated the situation to the legal courts.

Whippings

Apart from the problems of illegitimate children, loose women generally attracted the most unsavoury of characters to a village, like marauding tom cats. Such individuals presented a potential threat to the peace and order of the community. For these reasons, a quarter of women giving birth to bastards, and many of those deemed to be of a loose nature, were whipped through the market place, from one end to the other and back again, until their bodies were covered in blood. Such punishment was dictated by the state court, but only after they had been reported to the court by the clergy or sufficient parishioners. It was normally the role of the vicar or church warden to report such women and to recommend them for such punishment. The offenders would be stripped from the neck to the girdle, and the punishment took place at the peak time of the market place activity to ensure that as many villagers as possible witnessed the result of such transgression of the church-dictated moral standards. A Limpsham woman was whipped from eleven to midday. Joan, a Glastonbury lass, received the same punishment at the hands of Constable Whitleigh. Glastonbury was a popular spot for such punishments as it was considered, in the first half of the seventeenth century, to have more whores than any other Somerset town.

In the smaller villages, with no market place, the hour-long whippings by the parish officials took place through the main streets of the village. Agnes Bourman was flogged at West Buckland, Edith Parker at Weston Bampfield, Agnes Poole at Norton FitzWarren, many of these immediately after evening prayers. All of these cases were between 1610 and 1650. Repeat offenders would receive double the punishment, once in their home village and once in the nearest market town.

Clearly the fear of such punishment put tremendous pressure on the mother to name the father of the illegitimate child, and this would normally lead to marriage and the removal of the problem. By naming someone, if the authorities believed the accused was the father, then it took the pressure off the mother. Hence innocent victims would often be falsely accused.

Sometimes mothers would run away through fear of a whipping, but the punishment when caught was even worse, the punishment being doubled with at least two market place whippings or, as in the case of a Wiveliscombe girl, confinement in the workhouse where she was to be whipped on alternate days for the duration of her stay. A Wincanton girl who had produced several bastards was sentenced to three whippings, one at Wincanton and two at Bruton.

In one extreme case both the mother and father of an illegitimate child were flogged through the streets of Glastonbury 'until their bodies both be bloody', the extra punishment being the result of fornication on the Sabbath! As an extra attraction to the event, they were preceeded through the streets by two fiddlers to stress the fact that the base–born child was the result of sex resultant from dancing on a Sunday. On rare occasions, a couple could escape the flogging if the court was convinced that they were soon to be married.

A fine example of false accusation comes from the village of Crowcombe and involves a local girl, Elizabeth Kerle, who in 1671 was 'under examination'. She confirmed that she was with child and that she was unmarried. She also confirmed that the father of the child was George Clement of Bridgwater who had carnal knowledge of her body on just the one occasion, and that no one else ever had, and that she had met Clements at a 'gossiping' at Over Stowey. Three months later, under oath once again, she gave new evidence. The base born child had now arrived and she named the father as Henry Cole of Crowcombe, her own village. She also stated that he had carnal knowledge of her body on numerous occasions, and was the only one who could be the father. It became clear from her evidence that Cole had persuaded her to name the Bridgwater man and then to go to Wales and 'lose the child'. She could then return to Crowcombe and he would ensure she wanted for nothing as long as his name didn't get mentioned.

Friends in high places

Often it was the role of the church warden to report for trial cases of illegitimacy or illicit sex. Church wardens were usually elected for a year at a time. It has always been advisable to take care of who one tramples on the way up, since you may meet the same person on the way down. Perhaps it was with this in mind that a Durston church warden, Henry Bryant, refused to report a couple from his village for inappropriate behaviour. I suspect however that the man concerned was a close personal friend.

Mr Chead had returned home one day when, to his horror, he found his wife Joan in bed with George Chick. Chead went to the church warden to report the matter. This was the least he could do. Husbands whose wives had 'crossed the line' were considered to be cuckolds if they didn't keep their wives under control, and that could be punished. So Chead reported the offence but Bryant refused to act since Chead could not confirm that he had seen 'the thing in the thing', and hence there was insufficient evidence to prosecute. Now, this was in the days when just entering the house of a wife when her husband was away was considered proof enough of inappropriate behaviour. In the case of Chead, he had caught Chick actually in bed with his wife. Clearly Chick was a close personal friend of the church warden – or perhaps he had been visiting the same lady himself for similar reasons!

Some clergy were greater zealots than others and one Somerset parson who preached against the relaxation of attitudes towards sexual practices was excommunicated for meddling in marital affairs, such matters being the responsibility of the church court and not down to individual members. In Somerset, it was the courts, headed up by the archdeacon at Taunton and the Bishop of Bath and Wells, which attempted to control local moral behaviour. Within the community, pre-marital sex was accepted as the norm as long as a couple were recognised as having agreed to get married. The church, of course, held different views and it was the church wardens who were expected to report any transgressions, which included not only extra-marital sexual activity but also husbands and wives who were living apart, since this was liable to lead to unacceptable behaviour. For the church authorities, solid proof was not a requirement. Rumour and innuendo, on the basis of no smoke without fire, was quite sufficient to provoke action. A man visiting a lady's cottage late at night when her husband was away, or climbing over the back fence when there was a front door to be used, was immediately assumed to be guilty.

In 1650, the Puritan Commonwealth parliament introduced new laws under which the death penalty was introduced for incest and adultery. However, this was relaxed if the man was unaware that the woman was married or if the woman's husband had been absent for at least three years. Fornication, as a lesser offence, resulted in three months gaol – but a second offence carried the death penalty! These new laws moved some of the power away from the clergy, which perhaps was just as well since they were not without fault themselves.

At Martock, Elizabeth Flint was seen at the house of her brother James, destroying by fire what appeared to be the result of a miscarriage. It was believed that the local parson had seduced her and then cajoled her into taking a medicine to produce the miscarriage. Most villages would have a woman who understood and could provide such recipes.

Misbehaving vicars

William Webber, the vicar of Sampford Arundel, was recognised as a lecherous reprobate and a liar. For four years he unsuccessfully pursued the attentions of a happily married woman, requesting carnal knowledge of her body. The whole village knew what was going on and the vicar was banned from visiting the house concerned. He was humiliated and angry enough to seek revenge. He told the husband that the wife was working as a prostitute selling her favours to a particular parishioner. The vicar then pursued the woman, stalking her everywhere, hoping to find minute pieces of evidence which he could use to throw suspicion on her. He was carefully building a convincing case and ultimately the husband was persuaded of his wife's infidelity. As it happened, the husband was in debt to the vicar and the vicar decided it was time to call in the loan. However, he promised the husband that he would give him more time to pay if the husband threw the wife out of the matrimonial home for her infidelity.

It was time for the final part of the plan to fall into place. The vicar notified the wife that she should visit him to confess her adultery with a villager who the vicar had falsely accused. Fortunately the wife, husband and villagers were able to see through the vicar's devious plan. The couple were reconciled and the villagers had a whip round to settle the husband's debt. The vicar however had not given up and went to a village girl who was single and expecting a child, and instructed her to name the innocent husband as the father of the unborn child – but by now no one would believe anything the vicar said and he left the village in disgrace.

At Newton St Loe, the vicar George Bryant was more successful with his attempts to seduce his parishioners. Giles Cornish arrived home earlier than expected and was shocked to find the vicar in bed with his wife. Cornish's action was immediate. He decided to disgrace the vicar by taking him to court. The vicar however counter–attacked and threatened to take Cornish to court for similar behaviour with another woman.

The one-time vicar of Cutcombe also had his wicked way with a parishioner. He was a widower and in need of creature comforts. One of his parishioners was dying, slowly, and the wife was also in need of the same comforts. The vicar and the patient's wife began a lusty affair, sleeping together on a regular basis. The wife admitted later that she fully expected to marry the vicar once her husband had died, which conveniently he did a few weeks later. The affair continued and the vicar assured the widow that he would marry her. She became pregnant and the weeks dragged on, but with no sign of a wedding date being announced. Her suspicions as to his intentions were aroused and confirmed when he told her that he would not marry her, but instead give her £10 not to name him as the father. In fact, he supplied her with a list of three names from which she could choose any one to nominate as the father of his child. When the case eventually went to court, the magistrate sat there with gaping mouth, shocked as the story unfolded.

Musical mistresses – when the music stops!

The county archives provide ample evidence that the clergy of the early seventeenth century included a good number of lechers who took advantage of their privileged and trusted position. Robert Wolfall was the vicar of Westonzoyland from 1589 to 1610. During that time he and his son were accused of licentious and drunken behaviour. He was lucky to get away with it for as long as he did when you discover what he got up to. In 1607, Wolfall had to deal with Joan Venn who was living immorally with Thomas Creiden. He had the man removed and the woman punished. The punishment presumably wasn't too serious for within three weeks the very same Joan Venn had moved in with Wolfall.

It gets worse. When Wolfall heard that Elizabeth Bragge was playing around, he paid her a visit, the result of which was that she was led into the cider house and her dress went up as his trousers went down, and at the critical moment the lady's husband arrived. Could it get worse? Yes – his next victim was Susan Perfitt, his son's mistress. Wolfall complained that his son and Susan were living immorally and he, as the lad's father, had her removed from his son's house. So she moved in with Wolfall senior, to the annoyance of

Wolfall's wife who eventually insisted that the girl should leave. So the vicar passed her on to his neighbouring parson, John Symes. Well, it wasn't quite that simple. He actually swapped her for John Symes's mistress!

Susan Perfitt's next move was to the house of Margaret Agnis who was another mistress of the vicar. The incestuous relationship got even more complicated when Wolfall's son William moved in with Margaret Agnis as a result of which she gave birth to a child.

Now if the story isn't already sufficiently complicated, the plot thickens with Robert Wolfall advising John Hine, the parson at Greinton, that he should not allow a woman known for her lewd behaviour to reside at his parsonage for fear of what it could do for the reputation of the clergy in general, bringing discredit to vicars in particular. The advice was followed and the lewd woman departed – only to move into Wolfall's house in Westonzoyland. What an appetite this clergyman had. He also frequently employed London prostitutes and 'shopped locally' by providing business for the whores of Glastonbury!

Of John Gast, who was the curate and schoolmaster at Mark, we know that he wouldn't leave the girls alone. An account of his behaviour with a twelve-year-old girl, the daughter of a Mark husbandman, is documented in much detail but, in the interest of good taste, is inappropriate to a publication such as this. Suffice it to say that she screamed for help throughout the ordeal and then, having returned to the class, stared at her books for the next hour before plucking up the courage to run home to tell her mother of the ordeal.

David Jenkins was the curate at Locking in 1607. His vicar was senile and completely unaware of what was going on under his nose. Jenkins ended up in the stocks for liaisons with loose women, and ten years later married his mistress, despite already being married, and then had an eight-year affair with another one of his parishioners.

The clergy, in general, were fairly responsible when providing for the maintenance of their mistresses and illegitimate offspring, although one clergyman found it difficult when the sixth such child was on its way.

Wicked women of Wembdon

John Musgrave was the vicar of Wembdon, on the edge of Bridgwater, from 1624 to 1652 and was then sacked from the post. Over the course of those twenty-eight years he had taken at least five of his servant girls as lovers, having produced five illegitimate offspring between them. He was paying maintenance all over the county.

Wembdon Church c 1910

When his next mistress went off to Taunton pending the arrival of another bastard child, the county committee caught up with Musgrave for failure to pay what he owed to several parishes for maintenance. William Runson, the parish clerk, took three other men with him and raided Musgrave's home. There they found the vicar at four in the morning, up in the attic room in bed with yet another servant, Mary Smith, who was dressing as rapidly as she could. It seems that his parishioners forgave him for he was re-instated in 1660 and remained as Wembdon's vicar until 1671.

Meanwhile, in West Monkton, girls were queuing up to admit that John Williams, former vicar of the parish, was the father of their illegitimate offspring. At Pennard, farmer's wife Mary Colley took part in a four-year long affair with the parish clerk and on one occasion was actually caught in bed with him by her husband. But it didn't stop the affair – just brought it into the open. Of course some clergy lacked the charm or persuasion to seduce members of the congregation and so resorted to prostitutes or the local whore.

Ann Morgan, a prostitute in Wells had a sliding scale of fees for her customers. Soldiers had to pay two shillings and six pence, double what she charged the vicar. Occasionally when the troops were in town she would have to recruit four or five of her lady friends to help her out. Naturally once the vicar discovered what was going on the punishment swiftly followed. She was placed in the stocks in the market square and one of her customers was 'washed' in the palace moat.

Some whores were more discreet in their choice of clientele and a number of them served just the clergy, moving on from time to time from one parson or vicar to another, completing a circuit. Some women saw pregnancy as a way of entrapping a man to provide for their future financial security. Hence an unmarried mother would occasionally falsely name the father of the child as someone better to do than the actual father, a parson for example. A Thorne Coffin girl was persuaded to name Parson Hearne as the father of her child because he was better positioned financially to care for the child than a man named Chant who was the actual father. Occasionally false accusations backfired badly as in the case of the Somerset lass who accused the wrong person. He tried to kill her with a spade and had another go with a hatchet! In contrast, when Robert Cribb, a wealthy yeoman, got Ann Bishop pregnant, his friend Arthur Pulman, the constable for Martock, threatened to have her imprisoned, flogged and left to rot unless she denied that Robert Cribb was the father. In another case where the sexual act leading to a birth was actually witnessed by an older lady, the elderly witness was arrested and locked up to prevent her giving evidence. And just to make sure, her captors cracked her around the head, knocking her clear off her stool where she lay unconscious for the two hours that evidence was being presented. It will come as no surprise that the man who had knocked her unconscious was the father of the illegitimate child.

'Lock up yer wives, chaps. Vicar of Wembdon's come back!'
From a Somerset postcard circa 1905

3

Religious Sex Cult at Camberwick Green

From sex cult to *Trumpton*

In the quiet Quantock village of Spaxton, there is a house known as the Agapemone. In recent years, it has been used as a centre for the production of children's TV programmes such as *Trumpton* and *Camberwick Green*. But in a former life, its walls provided privacy for one of the world's most infamous religious sex cults, known as the Agapemonites. This community became the prototype for the many religious cults which existed in the twentieth century, with parallel accusations of brain-washing, abductions, dramatic rescues by family members and moral outrage from the established church and the popular press.

At the centre of the scandal was the Reverend Henry Prince, known within his community as 'The Blessed'. He would visit the nearby town of Bridgwater in a magnificent open-top carriage, purchased from the Queen Mother, drawn by four large horses, and protected on all four sides by outriders wearing purple livery. Enormous bloodhounds ran alongside his carriage and in the vanguard a trumpeter loudly proclaimed 'Blessed is He who cometh in the name of the Lord'. Clearly he was a flamboyant man, and he oozed with charisma. He was the type who would attract as many enemies as friends, but in the village of Spaxton, and the nearby town of Bridgwater, he was popular and welcome. He spent well with the local traders and paid cash on the nail. He made many gifts to the needy around the village. This was the public image of Prince – but behind the walls of the Agapemone, a different story was to unfold, and one which was to become a national scandal.

The Agapemone's Abode of Love
from the Illustrated London News *1905*

The Reverend Henry Prince

Henry Prince, born in Bath, embarked on a career in medicine. Having qualified at Guys Hospital, ill health interfered and his career took a change of direction – into religion. He took instructions at St David's College in Lampeter, West Wales, and soon became a religious zealot and an embarrassment to the college authorities. He founded a group of enthusiasts who called themselves the Lampeter Brethren. Claiming he heard voices in his head, he persuaded his followers to disrupt services and generally attack the college hierarchy, accusing them of submitting to the insinuations of carnal desire.

He had to go. The vice-principal contacted his friend the Bishop of Bath and Wells, pleading for his help. He asked if the bishop could find a quiet backwater of a village with a small church, deep in the countryside, where Prince could be 'exiled' and could cause no harm. The bishop knew just the place and in 1846 installed Prince as the curate for Charlynch church, just a stone's throw from Spaxton. The regular vicar was away on long-term sick leave and the congregation had been somewhat neglected. In fact it barely existed.

Charlynch and the Son of God

It was not the flying start for which Prince had hoped. With just a handful of elderly in his congregation, no amount of threats of hellfire and damnation was going to increase their numbers. Then he had a brainwave. At one of his services, he stopped mid-sermon and threw himself about the church as if possessed by some tormented spirit. The congregation were enthralled – especially when he declared himself to be the Son of God! He explained how he heard voices in his head, and realised from this that he had to be the embodiment of the Holy Ghost.

The next Sunday the usual congregation arrived, but this time with a few of their friends who wanted to see if the curate was about to repeat the performance – which, of course, he did. A week later, more fresh faces joined the flock including many from Bridgwater. Some of these were less savoury and certainly not there for religion. They filled up with drink in the town, and then rode out to Spaxton for a couple more at the Lamb, and then to Charlynch for the entertainment.

The Reverend Prince needed to sort out his congregation. First he held split services, one for the men, the other for the ladies. Then he separated his flock into Sinners and Righteous. With fixed, staring eyes he peered into the faces of the Sinners, pointing the accusing finger at each person in turn, defying them to attend his church again.

Then he smiled sweetly at the Righteous.

As the congregation settled down to a profile which more closely suited his needs, it became obvious that to be one amongst the righteous, you needed to be young, female and wealthy. Or old, female and wealthy if it appeared that you weren't destined to be on this side of the great divide for much longer.

Defrocked

Families became divided. Respected members of the community, labelled as Sinners, lost their status. The Bishop of Bath and Wells was called in once again to deal with the problem of the Reverend Prince. Not only was he required to investigate claims that Prince had declared himself to be the son of God, but there were several accusations regarding his carnal activities with members of his congregation. This time, the bishop was certain that he had found a lasting solution. Prince was defrocked and removed from the clergy for the south-west.

This left Prince without his clergy's stipend but that was no great problem. Prior to moving to Charlynch, he had married an elderly and wealthy lady, Martha. She was actually an older friend of his mother and he had originally married her in order that she could fund his way through college. She died and Prince inherited her fortune. With no delay, he married Julia Starkey, sister of the parish rector. Together they moved to Clare in Suffolk and there Prince started up all over again, building his flock over a period of two years, whipping the congregation into a frenzy, weeding out the sinners and encouraging the righteous who were, of course, wealthy spinsters. This time it was the Bishop of Ely who was called in to move the man on. It was once too often for Prince who decided that if the Church of England didn't need him, then he didn't need the Church.

The Nottidge sisters

Charming young tarts with the sweetest of lips,
Keep 'Glory's Dad' supplied well with 'the chips';
Mr 'Messiah' does nothing to scare 'em
But takes over the cash when they enter the harem.

Fleet Street satirical postcard – queuing for the vicar's harem

Amongst his recently lost congregation were five very wealthy, middle-aged spinsters, the Nottidge sisters. Between them they were worth £30,000 and three of them were persuaded to throw in their lot with Prince and they all moved to the south coast resorts of Brighton and Weymouth. It was there that the idea of the Agapemone (The Abode of Love) developed. It was to be a community with angels and archangels, a system within which Prince could promote or demote the members according to how well he favoured them, financially or lustfully, at the time. It would be a community where love was a spiritual emotion - albeit Prince certainly had an alternative and more physical agenda for his own purposes. To achieve his dream, he needed his own premises, away from the prying eyes of the inquisitive world. Such a vision required funding and the wealthy widows and spinsters of the coastal resorts were ideal targets and provided him with their fortunes.

He held revivalist meetings, with his Agapemonites whipping up support, in which he persuaded his listeners that judgement day was coming and now was the time to give up their wealth to support the Lord's work. He persuaded many that it was only by accepting himself as the messenger of God that they could be saved. The money rolled in and two hundred acres of land were purchased at Spaxton.

The Abode of Love

And so in the summer of 1846, a rather unusual group of people arrived at Spaxton, clearly well-to-do and rather grand in appearance. The development of the Agapemone had begun. First 15 foot high walls were erected, not unlike those of a Victorian prison, which served to provide privacy for those within and, when required, to prevent them from leaving. Within the walls were built a 20-bedroom house, chapel, gazebo, stables, cottages and conservatory. The chapel was luxuriously furnished with velvet sofas and Turkish carpets. Rather peculiarly a billiard table served as the altar.

The community members were well protected. Within the walls were enormous bloodhounds which maintained constant patrol. Only the local tradesmen had regular contact, and that was through a hole in the wall where they delivered their goods in return for prompt payment.

Prince's community continued to grow, mostly with young women, but he had included some of his gentlemen friends from his Lampeter Brethren days, and three of these he married off to the three Nottidge sisters. It appears the sisters had been somewhat bullied into these marriages which were to be purely spiritual unions, indeed the couples lived separate lives, men in one group of cottages and women in another. Only the young, single females lived in the main house with Prince.

A press man fails to gain entrance to the Agapemone

The eldest Nottidge sister, Agnes, objected strongly to the prospect of a celibate life and wrote to her youngest sister, Louisa, warning her not to become involved, knowing that Prince already had her as a target. Agnes was not to be a member for much longer. Prince discovered that she had betrayed him, by contacting her sister, and, it appeared, she was expecting a child and not by her spiritual husband.

Nonetheless, Louisa was persuaded to join the community and was lodged in a cottage at the Abode of Love. Some nights later, the customers at the Lamb Inn, adjacent to the community's grounds, heard screams as Louisa's two brothers attempted to 'rescue' her against her will. They dragged her outside and bundled her into a carriage which sped away into the night. It was a sad demise for Louisa. Her brothers had her declared insane and she was committed to a lunatic asylum. A year and a half later, word got through to Prince that Louisa had escaped the asylum and was in hiding in a London hotel. Arrangements were made to repatriate her to the community and she was met at Paddington Station. Unfortunately asylum officials were already there, waiting to pick her up and she was returned to the asylum. Prince, determined to arrange her release, made an application for her to be re-examined and she was declared sane. She immediately joined Prince at the Abode of Love, signed her fortune over to his keeping and spent the rest of her days in the community, protected by two personal bloodhounds, protection against any future attempted abduction.

Despite this early scandal, new members continued to flock to the community, perhaps with a sense of promise and adventure. The numbers swelled from sixty to two hundred, all of them completely under the control of Prince who lived the life of a king. Worshipped as a god, with a cellar full of the best wines, and surrounded by attractive and available females, who could ask for a more tempting life? But temptation was nearly his downfall.

The Great Manifestation

Whilst scandal had already followed scandal, the most bizarre episode was yet to come in 1856. Such was its impact that the world press was to report the story. Prince had proclaimed that it was his duty to extend love from heaven to earth. Virgins needed to be purified by the Holy Ghost, and he had already declared himself to be the Holy Ghost. So it was down to him to extend his love to the virgins – a purely spiritual event albeit with a very physical appearance. Nothing was left to the imagination as he carried out the Great Manifestation in front of his followers.

Prince would choose which virgins might benefit from his love. The young, spiritual potential brides were then paraded, draped in white, in front of the followers, including Prince's wife. After a careful examination of each one in turn, Prince chose Miss Zoë Paterson who had grown up in the community since she was a five-year-old. Now aged sixteen, she was a beautiful young woman. Her clothes were removed and she was lain across the billiard table which served as the altar. There, with the organ playing and hymns being sung, Prince deflowered the young virgin in an act which he declared as spiritual, a divine purification, but which many could only see as pure unadulterated sex. Some, who had once believed in him, now had grave doubts and threatened to leave the community, taking their money with them. Some did and they also took with them a story which was to hit the world's headlines. The press had a field day. The community became the centre of an international scandal and the people of Spaxton kept their mouths closed and tongues tight.

Eventually the attention of the press subsided and the community settled down, only to be disrupted by another upset. Zoë Patterson was pregnant. Prince declared this must be the work of the devil and unrelated to his purification. Others, perceiving a more conventional interpretation, left in droves. The 'purified virgin' gave birth, adding weight to the suggestion that Prince, after all, was not the immortal Holy Ghost, confirmation of which came with his death many years later. But meanwhile, the 'devil's daughter', Eve, grew up into a shy young lady within the Spaxton community, with Zoë taking her place at the right hand of the 'Beloved' as the first Bride of the Lamb.

Zoë was the first of many brides, which scandalised the local community causing the Agapemonites to withdraw further behind the walls of their community, shutting out the world at large. Their isolation simply added fuel to the speculation of the press leading to stories which were undoubtedly greatly exaggerated. But inside the walls, the middle-aged Prince lived for the next thirty years with his brides, enjoying games of billiards and the relaxed life of a recluse.

The Death of the Immortal One

Prince outlived most of his 'saints', adding further conviction to their belief in his immortality, until, of course, he in turn died in 1899 aged eighty-eight. But there were still those who believed in his immortality. They held séances to try, unsuccessfully, to make contact. And so his community had him buried, at midnight, under the lawn of the Agapemone, with his coffin interred upright so that he would be standing on the day of his resurrection. Others were to follow, all in unmarked graves.

A successor was required and the Reverend John Hugh Smyth-Pigott, a vicar in Clapton, had heard the news and put himself up for the job, declaring he had seen a heavenly light which told him what he needed to do. Prince's right-hand man, Douglas Hamilton paved the way and Smyth-Pigott was installed. Inspired by his predecessor's actions, he declared to his Clapton congregation that he was the reincarnated Son of God and off he went to Spaxton, but not before he had to be rescued by the police when events took an ugly turn outside of his Clapton church. The press were already onto his story and set off in hot pursuit to the Somerset village which served as home to the Agapemonites.

As in any successful takeover, the first function of a new 'chief executive' is to take stock of the assets. Smyth-Pigott's inventory showed an ageing community and so he announced that young, fresh blood was required – female, of course. Fifty young girls were recruited as a result of the campaign, each of them vetted by the now mature woman Eve Paterson. Smyth-Pigott already had a wife, and she was attractive enough, but he felt the need for a spiritual wife in addition, and Ruth Anne Preece was selected to be his Chief Soul Bride. She bore him three children, two boys and a girl called Glory, Power and Hallelujah!

Another scandal hit the headlines as the Church of England defrocked yet another vicar. Defrocking this one proved difficult. The Bishop of Bath and Wells, in his attempts to visit Smyth-Pigott, was

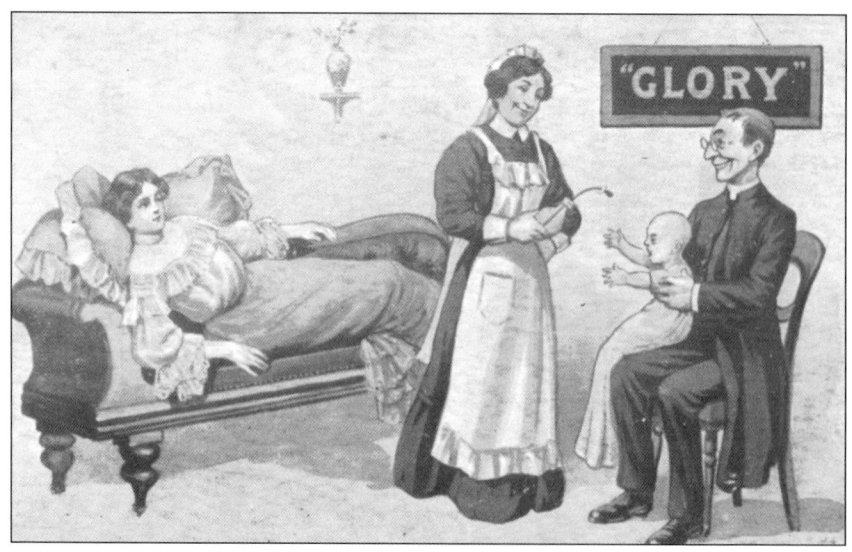

Beautiful Ruth on her couch doth recline
Whilst Nursey makes pap for the Infant Divine,
'The Lord' on a chair very cheerfully sits
And keeps 'Glory' quiet from getting the fits.

From a Fleet Street satirical postcard around 1905

welcomed with the news that 'The Messiah is away at present'. The press met with similar reactions and the people of Spaxton remained tight-lipped, returning the favours of decades of charitable acts by the Agapemone community.

Life settled down as the press lost interest and Smyth-Pigott brought a new style to the community, introducing a motor-car, a laundry, new livestock for the farm and building new cottages. Despite all this activity, he still found time to fulfil his role as the Heavenly Bridegroom, with sex being both his obsession and his driving force. His earthly and now neglected wife, busied herself with acts of charity which earned her the hearts of the people of Spaxton.

Smyth-Pigott died in 1927, signalling the beginning of the end of a community which had lasted over a hundred years. By 1929, the community had dwindled to 37, only three of whom were men. In its latter days, Sister Ruth took the helm until her death, aged ninety, in 1956.

In 1958, the Agapemone was sold to a private developer and converted into flats. No more secrecy surrounds the place. The chapel, where once virgins were deflowered on the altar, was turned into a puppet studio by a partnership who produced educational and light entertainment films for the BBC, programmes such as the innocent *Trumpton* and *Camberwick Green*. A greater contrast between past and present uses is hard to imagine.

Spaxton, meanwhile, has slipped back into its undisturbed and quiet way of life.

THE ABODE OF LOVE.
The Boots are here all in their proper position. But Glory!
Whatever's this latest Addition?

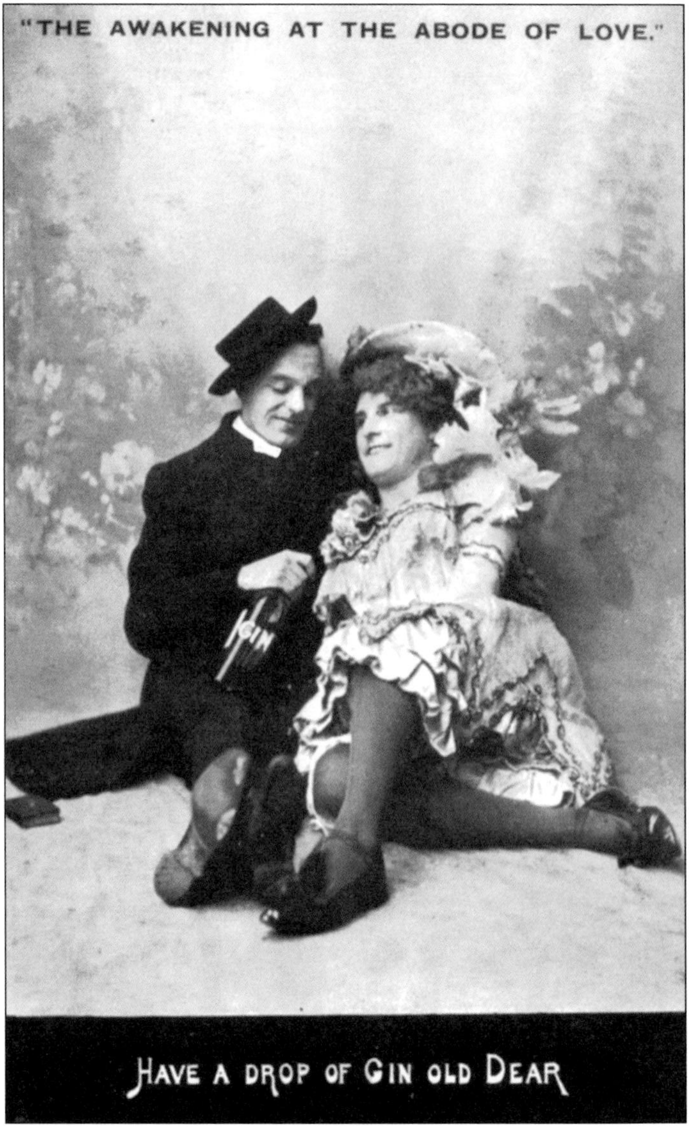

"THE AWAKENING AT THE ABODE OF LOVE."

HAVE A DROP OF GIN OLD DEAR

Births, Marriages and Deaths

Births

Church records provide a fascinating insight into the attitude towards illegitimacy across the centuries. At Baltonsborough, an illegitimate child in 1720 was christened Misfortune Pope! One at Tellisford in 1752 was christened Freelove Nash, as if to rub in the parent's misbehaviour. Then at Nether Stowey there was Temptation Brewer, and in adult life she lived up to her name, being prosecuted for leading an immoral life.

Perhaps one gentleman who should have sired far more children than he did was the nineteenth-century Somerset clergyman Cicero Rabbits. Maybe he met Elias Ferret who was around at the same time! One clergyman who did produce a small tribe of children was William Rich of Lydeard St Lawrence where a churchyard epitaph once recorded his many marriages. He was widowed eight times:

Beneath this stone in sound repose
Lies William Rich of Lydeard Close
Eight wives had he yet none survive,
And likewise children, eight times five;
From whom an issue vast did pour
Of great grandchildren five times four.
Rich born, rich bred, but fate adverse
His wealth and fortune did reverse,
He lived and died immensely poor
July 10th aged ninety four.

Marriages

Some get married more often than others – but not usually the vicar. However, George Hellier, one-time vicar of Broomfield, married and buried three wives, Ursula, Dorothea and Diana. A memorial in the church recalls 'Thrice married, thrice bereaved, I went to three funerals of wives; may the triune God assist these tears.' He didn't grieve for too long – he was soon on wife number four.

Sage and Onion

In Yatton on 12 July, 1762 there was the amusing marriage of Samuel Sage to Hannah Onion. No they didn't' chicken' out and the honeymoon wasn't in Turkey.

A marriage where we can definitely 'blame it on the vicar', is that of William Bacon and Mary Gadd. William was born in Sampford Arundel in 1725 and, as a fifteen-year-old, hired himself out, at Bridgwater Fair, to Farmer Tonkins from Stogumber. It appears that he failed to keep his passions under control whilst working in Stogumber and as the result of a one-night stand, Mary Gadd was expecting his child. In earlier chapters I have already dealt with the penalties for giving birth to illegitimate children and the financial burden on the parish. Needless to say the overseers of Stogumber were soon on William's case, pressurising him into marrying Mary. But he was having none of it. No amount of bullying was going to persuade him otherwise.

The overseers decided to try a change of tactics and arranged for the banns for the marriage to be called. The vicar was somewhat bemused since he knew, as well as the rest of the village did, that William was refusing to get married. The overseers pointed out to the vicar that the purpose of calling the banns was to see if there was any LEGAL reason for a couple not to be married. It had nothing to do with whether or not they wanted to get married. 'You call the banns, vicar, and leave the rest to us'.

Hoodwinked

The banns were called for the next three weeks and the overseers kept up their pressure on young William. On the third Sunday, they visited William and confessed that they had virtually given up. However, they would like one last chance to persuade him and wanted to keep it really friendly – so they all went down to the village pub where they paid for a jar of cider for William. They were surprisingly amicable and hinted at a possible arrangement. William, thinking that perhaps there was a financial incentive to be announced, listened attentively and supped another jar which was placed before him. And thus the meeting continued, with the overseers never quite getting to the point and William slowly succumbing to the effects of alcohol.

When he was in a completely drunken stupor, they dragged the poor lad up to the church where the vicar and Mary Gadd were waiting. Perhaps someone asked 'Do you want another pint, Billy?' and he answered 'I do'. And that was it. In a drunken stupor, totally unaware of what was going on, the poor lad was married.

The following morning he woke up in bed with Mary and must have been thinking 'Oh, no! I've done it again.' But Mary explained that they were now man and wife, not that he believed her. He had no recollection. Mary fetched the vicar and the vicar confirmed that he had married them the previous day. 'But I was drunk, vicar. I had no idea what was going on!' 'Well, I thought you looked a bit under the weather but you definitely said "I do" at the appropriate moment.' You just can't trust some vicars.

Bigamy

The calling of banns has a purpose, not least to ensure that someone isn't marrying for a second time whilst still married to the first wife. But that is exactly what happened in Somerton in December 1840. Charles Butt, born on the Isle of Wight, was a master mariner who in 1834 married Mary Field in Middlesex. However, he deserted his wife and eventually turned up in Somerton in the late spring of 1840. He described himself as a naval captain with an estate, timber forests, a mansion, farms and considerable assets in the shipping business. He was a charmer, aged twenty-nine, and soon had twenty-six-year-old Betsy Barnard under his spell. Seven months after arriving in Somerton, they were married. Then the truth leaked out, by which time Betsy was already expecting his child. Barnard was taken to trial at Taunton, found guilty of bigamy and sentenced to eighteen months hard labour. Naturally the marriage was null and void, and Betsy gave birth to an illegitimate child. She was fortunate to eventually marry Michael Dawe, a farmer from East Chinnock and with him raised a family.

Another bigamous relationship fell into the domain of the Reverend John Skinner at Camerton in 1807. Sarah Summer's husband had gone away to the East Indies as a soldier. Seven years later, he had still not returned and Sarah, granting her the benefit of the doubt, had presumed him to be dead. In the meanwhile, she had taken to living with a man by the name of Coward and it appears that she hadn't waited long after her husband had gone away because by 1807 she had four children by him. She asked the Reverend Skinner to read the banns for her marriage to Coward. Skinner initially declined, suggesting that she was already married and her husband may still be alive. She convinced the vicar that her husband was dead and the banns were read.

The day of the wedding arrived and she dressed up in her best, which was particularly nice for her husband to see her that way when he turned up just before the ceremony. He was really pleased to see her but was taken aback by the four children who accompanied the one child of his own. The story unfolded, they were reconciled but it only lasted a month. He disappeared to Timsbury and she eventually married Coward.

Of other weddings, Skinner wrote with unusual humour: 'There was a wedding by licence this morning ... This was to be kept very secret, and I perceived the reason, for the bride was already far advanced' and 'I had to marry a couple at half past eight, the bride Miss Short as round as a barrel, and according to custom, I suppose there will be a christening in the course of the honeymoon'. Of one Christmas wedding he wrote 'Smallcombe, who was married on

Christmas Day, and whose wife was brought to bed the same day, sent his child to be named, as they were afraid it will die'.

Wedding day fatality

A most unfortunate wedding was that of young Eleanor Lovell, the daughter of the rector of Bawdrip church, near Bridgwater. It was 1681 and the Reverend Edward Lovell had moved to the parish fourteen years earlier with his wife Eleanor and their two daughters, Mary and Eleanor. His wife and elder daughter Mary had both died. Eleanor, the daughter, and her father lived alone in the gloomy old rectory, mourning their loss. Then the rector died and Eleanor was on her own apart from a couple of servants.

The villagers did their best to make life easy for her but her grief was obvious. So they were all delighted when she fell in love and it was announced that she was to marry her cousin, also by the name of Lovell, a lad from Castle Cary. The whole village turned out to watch as the couple left the church. Even the bishop was there.

The adults made their way to Knowle Hall for the celebratory feast whilst young Eleanor stayed at the church to play for a while with the village children. They played hide-and-seek. It being Eleanor's special day, she was the first to be 'it', the first to hide. Eleanor chose an old chest which was stored in the vestry, just big enough to take her. She climbed inside and brought down the lid, unaware that the catch had snapped shut and she would be unable to escape if no one found her. We can only imagine her delight as she heard the children calling 'Come out, come out, wherever you are', and then their voices fading away as they moved further afield. Tragically, she then realised that her hiding place had become her tomb and she slowly slipped into unconsciousness through lack of air and quietly passed away.

Within the church at Bawdrip is a plaque inscribed in Latin. Part of it reads 'Lastly, Eleanor, the daughter, heiress of the family honour and estates, died June 14th, 1681. Her sorrowing husband mourned her, taken away by a sudden and untimely fate, at the very time of the marriage celebrations.'

Grave situations

Whilst funerals, by their very nature, are sombre occasions worthy of solemnity and the greatest respect, they nonetheless provide their own moments of humour from unexpected and bizarre episodes. One example came at the funeral of a local butcher when one of the chosen hymns was 'Sheep may safely graze'. And that wasn't played particularly well since the regular church organist was unable to attend and at the last minute the pub pianist had to be persuaded away from the nearby bar.

I only need to draw on my own experiences to provide further examples. At the funeral of an aunt, one of those who is no relation at all but who has always been close enough to the family to merit the title, I was at her house on the morning of the funeral as we awaited the hearse and mourners' cars. They duly arrived and we boarded the waiting black limousines to head off to the nearby church. As I sat in the car behind the hearse, I could hear the repeated unsuccessful whining from the car engine in front of us. The embarrassed driver of the hearse was unable to start the car.

A few minutes passed and it became obvious to all present that we were going nowhere. We stepped out of our limousine and wondered up to the driver in the lead car, asking if there was anything to be done. 'Yes' came his reply, 'can you give me a push. I'll see if we can bump start her.' So there we were, four of us at the back of the hearse, pushing and running as fast as we could until the engine of the hearse fired into action and 'Auntie' had been successfully kick-started on her final journey. It was a bizarre moment and I felt the echoes of that occasion when the same lady's brother died a few years later and just before Christmas. At the church service, the only space available to place the coffin was immediately beneath the Christmas tree. I remember standing there singing a hymn and inwardly smiling at the coffin resting there amidst piles of make-believe presents, all in their Christmas wrap, the coffin providing an impression of a gift missed during the wrapping process.

Then there was the funeral of a work colleague and old school friend. The interment was at a cemetery on a hillside. The cortege of mourners' cars followed the hearse in through the gates and up the hillside before peeling off to one side into a parking area. The hearse continued the short remaining distance up the hill. We alighted from the cars and walked towards the graveside and the now open-backed waiting hearse. Then we noticed that it was slowly rolling back down the hill. The handbrake had not been adequately put on and the hearse was picking up in speed as the caped vicar, the nearest person to the vehicle, began his dash towards the car. Coming up alongside, with his cassock flapping in the wind, like a caped crusader, he opened the door, leapt in and applied the handbrake, thus saving the situation.

At that moment my 'A' level knowledge of physics kicked in as I realised that although the hearse had come to an abrupt stop, it didn't mean that the coffin would. I closed my eyes as the horror of the moment struck, visions of the coffin shooting down the hill with the vicar leaping on board like a delinquent skateboarder, only to find on opening my eyes that all were safely gathered in. The widow turned to me and quietly said 'That's typical of him. Always has to have the last laugh'. And she was right. It was his kind of humour. To give an example of this, there was an occasion when we travelled up to Gloucester together where we worked through the night before driving back the following day. On the way home, we stopped at a 24-hour night club and restaurant, to get some breakfast. My friend had spent £8 on the fruit machines and won over £100. The following day when he put in his claim for our travelling expenses, he included the £8 under the heading of 'Entertainment' – no mention of his £100 winnings.

The biker who almost missed his own funeral

Yet more bizarre was an episode in early 2003 when Ronald Howell nearly missed his own funeral. The hearse on which he was travelling was pulled over by police on its way to Yeovil's crematorium. Ronald was seventy-four when he died and was a motorbike enthusiast. It had been his wish to be given a 'biker's funeral'. It's not uncommon.

Many bikers have declared that they wouldn't be seen dead in a car. Conveniently the Leicester-based Reverend Paul Sinclair provides the nation's only motorcycle hearse service and travels all over the country on his converted Triumph 900, with its side-car specially adapted to carry coffins. That special adaptation means that it is taxed as a car, rather like an open-topped sports car.

The motorbike hearse was travelling along the A303 as it approached Yeovil. Flowers rested on top of the coffin, along with Ronald's crash helmet. Riding pillion on the bike was the Reverend Sinclair, known as the 'Faster Pastor', without a crash helmet. Since the vehicle was taxed as a car, he didn't need one. But that didn't stop a policeman from pulling him in for not wearing a helmet. The vicar pointed out to the policeman that the vehicle was taxed as a car and showed the officer the tax disc. The vicar continued by explaining that vehicles over 410 kilograms do not require the wearing of a helmet. He also explained that they had a funeral to get to but the officer insisted. They were going nowhere until he had carried out the necessary checks. Then, perhaps somewhat insensitively, the officer took photos of the vehicle and the coffin. The vicar's only consolation was that Ronald's family members weren't there to witness the scene.

Finally released by the officer, the vicar opened up the throttle and sped off to the crematorium where he arrived with a minute to spare. One of the ironies of this bizarre episode is the fact that throughout his life as a biker, Ronald Howell had never once been stopped by the police – but they got him on his final journey. And he was also the only one involved who was actually wearing a helmet – albeit it was on top of the coffin.

Dung heap burial?

Needless to say, the authorities interfering with a funeral service is not a new phenomenon. In 1661, when the Quakers were being persecuted by the Anglican church, a group of Quakers were carrying a coffin to their burial ground at Limington when they were attacked by Thomas Horsey, the rector of East Lydford, and his gang of men.

Horsey and his gang threw the coffin down to the ground and demanded six shillings and eight pence to carry it away. If the Quakers failed to pay up, then Horsey declared that he would have his men take it away and bury it in his dung heap. After two days waiting in Lydford church, the body was eventually buried in the churchyard and the rector had protected one element of his income.

The only winners were the solicitors

It is a sad fact of life that after many funerals, the arguments begin over the inheritance and previously close families can be rent asunder. Such was the case with Gabriel Goodman who purchased the manor of Kilmersdon in 1659. Twenty years later, he had passed away and his will was read. Having no sons, the estate was left to his two daughters. However, he knew them well enough to know that they would argue over the inheritance and so he left a request in his will that the executors of the will should try to persuade his daughter Mary to give her half to her sister Sarah, with the rider that if she did not, she would be unworthy of what had been left her in the first place.

It didn't take long for the arguments to begin. One sister declared that half the estate was hers, because the will said so, and the other sister declared that it wasn't because their father had said she was unworthy of it. The case was bitterly fought and the legal fees were so high that, by the time the dispute was settled, there was nothing left over which to argue.

Putting on weight

There is a lovely story, with no proof that it ever happened, of the Somerset widow who was holding the post-crematorium wake at the family home. The open-topped urn had been placed centrally on the drawing-room table and the room was filling with friends and family from far and wide. Drinks were passed around, a finger buffet was slowly being devoured, and the smokers in the room were helping themselves to the fine cigars which had previously belonged to the deceased but which the widow had placed for her husband's friends to enjoy.

A short-sighted, hard-of-hearing uncle was puffing away on a large Corona, thinking he was flicking the ash into an ashtray, but mistakenly flicking it into the urn containing the deceased's ashes. A deathly hush fell on the room as the mourners, with the exception of the aged uncle, realised what was happening. The widow entered the room, instantly spotted what was going on and defused an otherwise embarrassing moment as she commented 'I see he's putting on weight again!'

A pauper's funeral

Perhaps the saddest of funeral stories is that told by Llewelyn Powys, son of the vicar of Montacute, in his *Scenes from a Somerset Childhood*. It concerns the pitiful life of Nancy Cooper of Montacute. Her mother had died when Nancy was still very young and her father followed her while Nancy was still a young girl. However, she was well-to-do having inherited her parents' cottage and a number of freehold properties. Misfortune struck when she fell in love with, and married, a local lad-about-town who soon wasted her fortune and then left her penniless and with an infant child as he sailed off to Canada, as far as she knew never to return.

Coming from a fairly well-to-do family, Nancy was unaccustomed to hard work and she was too proud to enter the workhouse. She adopted the life of a vagabond, tramping the lanes and byways, sleeping in sheds, under hedges or anywhere that would provide her and her child with some respite from the elements. With the passing years, her face became weather-beaten, lined with deep furrows; her clothes bore the patches which held the rest together; her boots were permanently encrusted in mud. She had the image of a poor lady from a fairy-tale who perhaps would turn out to be a fairy godmother – but her life had no fairy-tale ending.

Tom Richards was a hard-working, hard-drinking Montacute quarryman. He originated from Stoke-sub-Hamdon which was where he was gainfully employed, and where he would spend many an hour at the Prince of Wales public house. At the end of a heavy night's drinking, he would often sleep in a shed which acted as a lean-to at a nearby lime kiln. On one night, when he felt fit enough to complete the walk home, he was passing through Stoke Wood when he thought he heard a sound from the far side of a huge beech tree. Quietly walking around to investigate, he discovered Nancy Cooper scraping out a hollow in which to rest for the night with her child. It was a pitiful sight. Tom, out of kindness, offered her his bed for the night but she was understandably reluctant. He knew she would not give in and so he told her that if she would not take shelter with him, then he would stay with her to ensure she came to no harm.

In time they became an item. She moved in with Tom and became mistress of his little cottage. They started a family and life was improving for Nancy, no longer a vagabond. They were devoted to each other but tragedy was waiting around the corner. Tom was taken seriously ill and was unable to work. Living immorally as an unmarried couple, they had disqualified themselves from poor relief. Tom became so ill, that he was obliged to enter the workhouse infirmary and there, after several weeks, he died. As a pauper, he was to be buried in his home parish of Stoke-sub-Hambon.

On the day of the burial, Nancy waited outside the doors of the workhouse, her boots polished shining black and sporting a bonnet befitting the occasion. The horse and cart bearing the coffin emerged from the workhouse and Nancy followed in its wake as the one and only mourner. They passed through Preston at a pace appropriate to the solemnity of a funeral cortege. As the hearse reached the bottom of Preston Hill, the driver and his assistant, keen to get this low-paid work out of the way, picked up the pace. Nancy ran behind, struggling to keep up with the faster moving vehicle. By the time they reached Montacute, this pitiful woman was breathless and soaked with sweat. But loyally she kept running as her legs weakened. Her estranged husband, now returned from Canada, stood outside the Phelips Arms with his drink in his hand, barely taking any notice of the passing spectacle.

Inevitably Nancy fell behind the pace and by the time she reached Stoke it was all over. The vicar had gone, and the grave diggers were just finishing the filling of the grave. Exhausted, Nancy collapsed across the freshly-filled mound, bitterly sobbing as she gasped for breath, all energy sapped from her body. The only words she heard were not those of comfort, but those of the grave diggers asking her to hurry up as they had to lock the gates before they left. 'Oh death, where is thy sting!'

In the years that followed, Nancy reverted to the life of a vagabond. She would dance for pennies in front of the village boys, doing a jig and always singing the same song. Her boots once again were permanently encrusted, her clothes more patched than ever, her face ever more deeply lined and weathered. Frequently she would visit Tom's grave, scattering it with the coloured leaves which collected in the creases of her clothes. Her daughter Betsy followed in her footsteps, living the life of a vagabond. She too died in the Yeovil workhouse.

Plenty of ale – but no friends or relations

The funeral of Tom Richards had the simplicity that Samuel Purlewent was seeking for his own funeral. Samuel was a well-known attorney-at-law who died in London in 1792, but he wanted to be buried at Weston on the outskirts of Bath. He wanted a simple funeral with no friends or family, no grand exit. His instructions were that his coffin should be carried to Somerset, but not in a hearse, just any old vehicle with no parade or coach to attend. His coffin was to get to Somerset as quickly as possible but at a cost not exceeding £25. He then wanted six poor people of Weston to carry his coffin to the grave, whilst six other local men and six local women attend the grave where he was to be buried at 12 noon. Each of the 18 attendees was then to be given half a guinea (52.5p) and taken to the Crown Inn where they were to be fed on good boiled ham, a dozen fowls, sirloin of beef and plum pudding. The church clerk and sexton were also welcome to join the feast. He concluded his wishes with the instructions that all in attendance were to be happy and really enjoy themselves. There was to be no weeping, crying or snivelling – as no good could come of it neither for the deceased nor the survivors. And 'No friends or relations whatever' were to attend!

Executions

None of us like going to funerals but pity the poor vicar who has to make such a regular appearance. In the line of his duties, he will grow accustomed to such occasions, and becomes a tower of strength through that experience. But the same cannot be said of another duty which vicars were occasionally called upon to perform, presiding at executions. The vicar, for example, would always be present at the burning of a witch, but just once in a while a woman would be burned for a different crime, and the vicar still had to attend.

Such was the case in 1753 with nineteen-year-old Susannah Davis of Chilton Trinity. In March of that year it had been a joyous occasion when she married John Bruford at Durleigh church, near Bridgwater. John was from West Monkton, near Taunton and his mistake was in marrying a woman whose loyalty would last no more than a few weeks. Within two months, she had found another lover and had poisoned her husband by mixing sufficient arsenic to kill twenty men into the medicine he was taking. After four days of absolute agony, he departed this world.

Susannah was taken to trial and found guilty. On 3 September, she was taken to Cure Green near Wells, drawn on a sledge. There, wearing a black gown and matching hood, she was taken to the stake. For half an hour the vicar prayed with her as the faggots of wood were placed around the stake, until finally she mounted a stool, prayed out loud, begging her Lord to receive her soul, and then she dropped the black handkerchief, the signal that she was ready to meet her maker. She was then 'turned off', a euphemism for being strangled, as barrels of pitch were added to the bonfire and the whole collection of material set ablaze, an intense fire burning for about an hour. Later, once the ashes had cooled down, her diminished remains were collected up in a small coffin for burial.

Some twelve years later, Mary Norwood of Axminster met a similar fate at Ilchester. She too wore a black dress but hers was soaked in pitch to aid the cremation. Again, she was strangled immediately before burning, and again the vicar was there to see her through her final moments.

Church Ales and Riotous Revels

Both churches and local communities encouraged fairs, fêtes and carnivals as fund-raising ventures. For the churches, 'church ales' were a popular money maker from as far back as mediaeval times. Special ales, normally strong ones, were brewed in nearly every parish and then sold in the Church House or church yard. The profit made was known as church ale. In 1595 Philip Stubbs wrote

'which mault being made into very strong ale or beer, is set to sale, either in the church or some other place. If all be true which they say, they bestow the money which is got thereby for the repair of their churches and chapels; they buy books for the service.'

So church ales were very popular at parish level, and encouraged by the parson and his church wardens, for whom they provided a regular source of income. However, some of the gentlefolk viewed church ales as an excuse for drunken behaviour and the year after Philip Stubbs made his remarks, Sir Francis Hastings left money to various Somerset churches but on the understanding that:

They never use again theyr churchales, to the prophaning of the Lorde's Sabaothe, the abusing of his creatures in drunkenness and ryott, and the corrupting of youth by training them up in gaminge and lascivious wantonness and sundry other disorders.

Various revels took place, on saints' days in particular, and these were another source of income for the church. However, these revels were frowned upon by the Puritans. Philip Stubbs, in his 1583 publication *The Anatomie of Abuses* referred to the dancing which took place at these revels:

Dancing, as it is used in these days, is an introduction to whoredom, a preparative to wantonness, a provocative to uncleanness, and an introite to all kinds of lewdness… For what clipping, what culling, what kissing and bussing, what smooching and slabbering of one another, what filthy groping and unclean handling is not practised everywhere in these dancings… and showed forth in their bawdy gestures of one another.'

Did the bells ring for you?

OK, so he didn't like dancing! But he makes a very strong case as to how dancing leads to touching and touching leads to – well, let me use an example from Broomfield Fair where a Taunton man had enjoyed a really good time and had partnered up with a willing young lass. When the dancing was over, they 'smooched and slabbered' and found themselves in a heavy caress against the pole around which the dancing had taken place. It was a big pole, as strong as a tree and provided strong purchase as the lass backed up to it, lifted her skirts and allowed the Taunton man to satisfy his carnal desires. However, choosing the dancing pole instead of a tree proved to be an embarrassing mistake. As their bodies rhythmically pulsed against the pole, they were unaware of the ringing of a bell until, as their passion increased, so the ringing increased in volume and pace, as if in time which their passion, reaching a frenetic and climactic finish. It was then that they realised it was the dancing pole which they had chosen in the dark and that at the top of the pole was a bell. The inquisitive crowd which had gathered were much amused!

Meanwhile, in Yeovil, the churchwardens came under investigation because they kept the church house doors open well beyond midnight and allowed the town's young lads and lasses to dance and drink. Worse still, on one occasion they allowed a drum-led procession of minstrels and dancers to hold an outrageous revel. When the church hierarchy threatened to stop such practices, the church wardens declared that the following year the revel would double in size and they would drink twice as much.

At Merriott, in the sixteenth century, proper behaviour was taken very seriously. It was declared that thieves should be hanged at the gallows, and playing unlawful games or failing to go to church should be punished with the stocks or pillory. At the same time the church wardens were discovered to be selling the church treasures without consent. By the eighteenth century only church-going paupers were permitted to receive poor relief and the church wardens were using beer from the local pub instead of the communion wine, and the curate ended up being so drunk that he had to be stopped from cutting off part of his hand to feed his dog! By the nineteenth century, the Merriott church was busy raising funds to pay for their paupers to emigrate which provided a more lasting solution to the perennial problem of paupers.

Banned – anything that's fun

The outcome was almost inevitable. The local magistrates introduced a county-wide ban on all bull-baiting, bear-baiting, church ales, clerks' ales, and all other kinds of ales. The ban was clearly unpopular. At Poyntington in South Somerset, Sir Edward Parham promoted a church ale with bull-baiting and morris dancing in order to 'get the love and affection of the common people' on the grounds that such festivals promoted 'love and familiarity amongst neighbours'. Needless to say, the ban didn't last for long.

It is ironic that within the church establishment, it was the same bishops who demanded that tithes should be raised who also banned the church ales. Revels and church ales helped the local churches to raise the money required. At St Cuthbert's in Wells, a new bell was required and they requested special dispensation from the ban to raise the money. The bishop was adamant – no church ale. The dean defied him and a fair was held with morris dancers, stick walkers, and a pageant including George and the Dragon, Robin Hood and the Sultan of Egypt, each of whom mocked the tyrannical bishop. This rivalry between the bishop and the dean lasted for years and at one time they actually excommunicated each other!

The banning of the church ales in the Elizabethan period was followed by the Puritan days of the early seventeenth century. And if we believe that this was a period during which high moral standards applied, then a study of that period reveals perhaps even greater lechery, even amongst the clergy as other chapters reveal.

Bring back the revels

By the eighteenth century, revels were back in fashion. In 1799, the Reverend Richard Warner was collared at Culbone Revel by an aged blacksmith who insisted on telling him how he had overcome his gambling addiction at the same revel some forty-five years before. He was drunk at the time and had lost all of his money gambling on the results of skittle competitions. Conscious of the fact that his wife was in bed at home, and close to giving birth, he knew he was in deep trouble when he got home if he failed to redeem the situation. Foolishly, with hindsight, he borrowed a guinea (£1.05) from a friend in order to win back his accrued losses. Needless to say, in his drunken state, things went from bad to worse. He lost another five shillings. Desperate, he went down to the stream, ducked his head under the cold water and left it there until he felt he was beginning to sober up and then returned to the skittles. With a clear head, he bowled straight and true and won back his losses and enough to repay his debt. But he never gambled again.

Culbone has a particular claim to fame in that it possesses the smallest parish church in England at just 35 feet long and with a wagon roof, single spire and two bells. Being in such an out-of-the-way place, the villagers would make do and mend as best as possible. Hence, the bell rope was not made of the conventional material but instead was made from woven hay bands. One night, to the amazement of the villagers, the bell was being tolled frantically, as if Napoleon himself were invading. They lit their lanterns and rushed to the church to hear what dire news may be awaiting them, only to find that an ox had found its way into the bell tower and was eating its way up the bell rope.

Hunting Parsons

In the churchyard at Montacute can be found the grave of John Scott who served for many years as a huntsman to a Montacute squire. The epitaph on his grave reads:

> *Here lies John Scott!*
> *It was his lot*
> *A huntsman bold to be*
> *He loved his can*
> *Like any man,*
> *And drank like a fish in the sea.*

To this epitaph the Bishop of Bath and Wells had the additional lines added:

> *And now, God wot,*
> *He has got his lot.*

The anti-hunting Bishop Phillpotts

There is just a hint here of the bishop's disapproval of hunting, or at least of the amount of time his clergy were spending hunting rather than performing their clerical duties. Henry Phillpotts, who was born in Bridgwater in 1788, became the Bishop of Exeter and in that role was a strict disciplinarian and had little time for clergy of a wayward nature. This was unfortunate since West Country vicars were particularly wayward. In Devon it was estimated that there were once over a hundred vicars who hunted. Twenty parsons even kept their own packs of hounds. One parson would cancel Sunday service if he was hunting and another, who also enjoyed shooting, would close his church for three months in the shooting season. The situation was much the same in Somerset and with the greater part of Exmoor in the county of Somerset, most of the Devon huntsmen rode to the hounds in Somerset as much as on their own side of the border. Red Deer and foxes are no respecters of political boundaries.

Shortly after Phillpotts moved across the boundary into Devon, he was driving through the county when a fox hunt went galloping by. Commenting on the number of riders wearing black coats, rather than red or green, he asked if those concerned were in mourning. The chaplain, his fellow traveller replied that 'No. They are members of the clergy. Their only bereavement is not to be wearing the pink.' In those days Somerset's parsons were hunting on anything from three to six days a week.

Exmoor black game shooting 1885 print by R M Alexander

Phillpotts decided that one of the first vicars he needed to sort out was the Reverend Froude who lived at Knowstone in Devon where he owned considerable land and had a significant private income. He also had a mafia-like gang of men who worked for him as beaters, errand boys and general henchmen, spending as much time in prison as out. They terrorised the locals, burning ricks and stealing sheep. The locals became so enraged that they tried to set fire to the vicarage and someone even fired a shot into the parson's bedroom, shattering a mirror.

Froude owned a wonderful pack of hounds and with these hunted three days a week, shooting on three others and occasionally holding a Sunday service. Phillpotts had considerable difficulty arranging to meet Froude and had to resort to written communication. When he enquired as to how many parishioners were being prepared for confirmation, Froude's reply was delivered on the back of a scrap of paper which, on the reverse side, had a list of hounds which had distemper. His response was that no one was ready for confirmation since not one of his parishioners could recite the Lord's Prayer backwards!

Froude was renowned for his practical jokes such as on the occasion when Dick Gathercole, a farm labourer from Dulverton, paid a surreptitious visit to Mary, one of Froude's maidservants, a young attractive lass. She had given Gathercole the tip off as to when her master was least likely to be around and as to how he could sneak into the house unnoticed. Unaware that Froude had twigged what was going on, Gathercole arrived and was let into the kitchen. Clenched in each other arms, they panicked when they heard Froude's footsteps approaching. The girl, perhaps foolishly with hindsight, bustled her lover into a large walk-in furnace, next to the kitchen range, where beer was brewed. No harm could be done, since there was no fire lit. Froude twigged immediately what had happened and instructed Mary to light the fire and be quick about it. He had brought some young pups with him which needed to be warmed up for fear that they would die of the cold. Mary obeyed, somewhat reluctantly but Froude was insistent. Soon there was a roaring fire and the pups were warming up nicely – so was the hidden visitor who was close to being roasted alive. Froude's knowing grin grew wider and wider as the maid's face coloured up with embarrassment and fear. The inevitable happened and the part-roasted would-be lover sprang out of the furnace, took one leap towards the mocking Froude, threw a single punch and knocked Froude to the ground.

Another practical joke from this Exmoor vicar came at the end of a day's hunting when Jack Babbage, who looked after the horses, took Froude's horse into the stables but then went into his accommodation to change his clothes before returning to bed down the horse for the night. Froude, who was by now indoors entertaining two visitors, took the opportunity of Babbage's absence from the stable to put his practical joke into place. He locked the stable door and then went back to his guests, knowing Babbage would be unable to brush and bed down the horse. Babbage, on his return, realised Froude was up to one of his pranks. He fetched a ladder, climbed up into the hay loft, which was over the horse's stable, prised up two planks from the floor of the loft, and lowered himself down into the stable. There he groomed the horse, gave it hay and water, and put down fresh bedding. All the horse's tack was wiped down and hung in place on the stable wall. Babbage then climbed back into the loft, nailed the planks back down, climbed down the ladder and put it safely away.

Froude returned later with his two friends to complete the practical joke and called for Babbage. 'Jack, come and show my friends how well you take care of my horse after a day's hunting.' said Froude. 'Sorry, master. Can't be done. The door appears to locked.' replied Babbage. Froude, grinning with expectation, produced the key. Babbage opened the door and the foursome stepped inside. Once Froude had recovered his dropped jaw, he gave a smile and suggested that perhaps it was time Jack joined them for a drink.

When Bishop Phillpotts later tried to visit Froude in person, Froude had prepared a trap. A hole had been dug in a stream into which Phillpotts's carriage sank. On a later visit, he actually managed to reach the vicarage and was told that the vicar had typhus. At that point, the bishop gave up trying and moved his attention to the Reverend Jack Russell whose name has been immortalised in the terrier breed developed by himself.

Parson Jack Russell

Parson Russell also lived across the border at Swimbridge in North Devon and loved to hunt on Dartmoor and Exmoor. He especially loved to hunt around the 'Doone Valley' and in 1879 invited the Prince of Wales, later to become Edward Vll, to hunt with him there. It became one of the most famous days in local hunting legends. A crowd of 15,000 people arrived and 1500 of them were mounted. Arthur Heal took the hounds over to Hawkcombe Head from their Exford kennels. Just before midday the honoured guests arrived, the prince and Claude Luttrell from Dunster Castle, and the party moved on to Culbone Stables where the prince ate bread and cheese, still mounted on horseback. The locals treated him with the greatest of respect, referring to him as 'Master Purnce'.

If local legend is true, then when the hunting party moved off, Parson Russell and a gentleman called Mr Snow were in the vanguard with the prince. Heading towards Badgworthy Water, the ground underfoot changed from heather to grassy sedge. As the party of three cantered towards the changing terrain, Russell and Snow, as if instinctively, peeled off to the right leaving the unaware prince continuing straight ahead into a peat bog. Within seconds, the prince's horse was up to its chest in the stinking mire. Fortunately the bog was small and the prince remained in his seat. The horse scrambled its way out as a local farmer stated the obvious

with 'Tis 'eavy goin' rown yer, Mister Purnce' bringing a smile to His Royal Highness's face.

At the end of a fine day's hunting, the stag was brought to bay mid-stream in Badgworthy Water and there the prince himself despatched the stag with Arthur Heal's hunting knife. That evening an incredible rumour spread like wildfire through the gentlemen's clubs in London. Fleet Street was abuzz as it frenetically struggled to discover the truth behind the rather ambiguous telegram that 'The stag was killed in the Doone Valley. The Prince slit his throat.'

Whilst Parson Jack Russell had the respect of the prince and vice versa, the same did not apply between Russell and the bully-boy Reverend Froude. Russell was much respected as a parson and was an eloquent orator. He detested the foul language used by the Reverend Froude and on one occasion, openly criticised Froude for it in front of numerous other huntsmen. On the way home, Froude ambushed Russell in one of those high-banked narrow lanes common to parts of Exmoor. He lashed Russell with his riding crop, drawing blood. Russell leapt from his horse and wrestled Froude to the ground where he pinned him down, demanding an apology. The altercation was interrupted by another huntsman on his way home and the two quietly rode off.

Jack Russell knew his hounds well, knew Exmoor like the back of his hand and could even recognise different foxes. In 1845 he was requested by an Exford farmer to hunt a group of young foxes which had wiped out the farm's flock of geese. Two were chased and killed. A third, somewhat grey in colour being the older dog fox, led them a merry chase and escaped after a 12 mile hunt across some of the wildest parts of the moor, having run through gorse too dense for the hounds to follow. Some months later, at another hunt meet, a fox was flushed out and Russell declared it to be the same fox which had got the better of them all those months before. His fellow huntsmen found it hard to believe that anyone could recognise individual foxes, especially when this one was 12 miles from its apparent home turf. The chase began, taking them from Yard Down to Sittaborough, onto

Simonsbath, the Warren and Badgworthy Water up to Gallon House, over a boundary fence where few could follow and right back to the covert near Exford from where the sly old fox had been flushed out several months earlier. With that the heavens opened and the rain washed away any scent trail which the hounds might have been able to follow.

Parson Jack Russell was still hunting in his eighty-second year but back to Bishop Philpotts and Russell in his earlier years. Phillpotts paid Russell a visit and was met with better grace than when he met Froude. The bishop enjoyed the visit with this eloquent gentleman. He asked Russell to give up his pack of hounds. Now a huntsman and his hounds become very close. This was a cruel thing to request but Russell had to respect his bishop's request. He agreed but declared he could not deceive the bishop – he would give them to his wife.

Moralists may well argue that it is wrong for the clergy to hunt. I doubt if those same moralists would argue that it is wrong for a vicar in a mining area to go down a coal mine, or to enter a shipyard. Good vicars, who recognise their calling as a mission, will integrate into the community and in that way 'touch the flesh' with the many who rarely if ever enter a church. Riding with the hounds when serving as a country parson should, perhaps, be viewed as necessary for the mission.

Reverend Joseph Jekyll

Another contemporary of Russell and Froude was the Reverend Joseph Jekyll. He was the vicar at Hawkridge, another Exmoor village on the Somerset side of the border. He was a man who didn't suffer fools easily and had a quick tongue in his armoury as the Duke of Beaufort discovered. Now the Duke apparently had been at a fairground and had a go on the Aunt Sally, a game somewhat like a coconut shy but the target is the model of a woman. Now something went seriously wrong, I know not what, but the episode became a serious embarrassment to the Duke and the story was told across the nation. It was just after that episode that the Duke and his hounds visited Somerset to join a fox hunt in the parish of Hawkridge. The Duke was a particularly arrogant man, not of a courteous or polite nature whatsoever. Parson Jekyll was riding well with the hounds, indeed better than the Duke himself who in anger at being upstaged cried 'You black-coated parson. Go home to your parish!' to which Jekyll replied 'This is my parish. Go home to your Aunt Sally!'

Another incumbent of Hawkridge-cum-Withypool, around 1805, was Parson John Boyse who kept a detailed journal of his time there. It reflects admirably on how hunting was given greater attention than matters of national importance. For example, he tells how 'a glorious battle was fought off Trafalgar in which the great Lord Nelson fell' in little more detail than that just quoted. However, describing his hounds he records 'Their colour generally hare-pied, long ears, deep muzzles, large throats. In tongue they were perfect; when baying the deer they might be heard at immense distance.' It's easy to see where the parson's priorities lay!

Reverend Gerard Tiarks

Loxton, in North Somerset, was well blessed when Gerard Tiarks was appointed its rector in 1875. He was loved and respected, and was a true huntsman. He even had a hunting lodge built in the village in addition to his home. Perhaps the most quoted episode of his career in the village comes from a day's hunting. He was riding alongside another huntsman when his companion's horse threw him into a deep rhyne, beneath the surface of which the rider momentarily disappeared. Coming back to the surface, coughing and spluttering somewhat, the unseated rider looked up at the still mounted rector and asked 'I didn't swear did I, parson?' Tiarks replied 'Must admit, I didn't hear you. But there were some uncommonly large bubbles coming to the surface!'

Tiarks' nephew, Herman Tiarcks, was another keen huntsman and published *Hunting Reminiscences*. He was an exceptionally tall man, being very long in the leg, and certainly believed in reincarnation for in his book he wrote:

When a sportsman dies, he doesn't go to heaven or hell, but just lives life over again in someone or something else's bod ... If ever when I am gone, a great long-legged fox is found in the neighbourhood, I hope the master or the huntsman will give him the benefit of the doubt if he goes to ground.

At Cloutsham Farm, near Porlock, hunting clergy were distinctive in their black coats

From the Illustrated London News *1899*

Get you next time, vicar!

But to more recent times. One time vicar of Holford, the Reverend Rex Hancock, who has now retired to Porlock, is well known in hunting circles. His father was the pre-war master of the Devon and Somerset Staghounds. During the war it was his mother and two other ladies who looked after the hounds. Hunting was in his blood and at one time he served as a hunt chaplain. Once during Sunday lunch with members of the Beaufort hunt, he was asked what he would have liked to have been if he had not been a huntsman. He replied that he would like to have been a clergyman! Now well into his seventies, Rex Hancock's hunting days are over as the result of an injury. He broke his leg at a funeral. As he was being stretchered out, the undertaker looked at him, smiled and whispered 'Get you next time'.

7

Cadfael's Successors

Whatever walk of life we tread, we all need a diversion, a hobby, a pastime. In the previous chapter, I focussed on the hunting parsons of Somerset. The village of Holford could once boast the 'Cowboy vicar' who was famous for appearing everywhere dressed in cowboy boots and wearing a ten-gallon hat. He is well remembered as something of an extrovert, even appearing a number of times on TV. Others, perhaps following in the footsteps of Cadfael or Father Brown, enjoyed their roles as amateur sleuths. One of those was the Reverend Thornton whose dominion covered much of Exmoor.

The Reverend Thornton

It was a brand new role when William Thornton arrived in Somerset, the first ever vicar for the parish of 'Exmoor', having a territory which covered one of the bleakest and yet most beautiful parts of England. He was an intelligent man, well suited to the needs of a far-flung community with diverse needs. It was his investigative mind which led to his recognition as one of the great vicars of his time, when his research and detection skills led to a father being captured and punished for the murder of his daughter.

It happened near the village of Simonsbath, deep in the heart of Exmoor. A riverside walk along the Barle leads to Landacre Bridge and Cow Castle. Along the route, one will find the remains of the Wheal Eliza Mine. Mining started here in 1846 and for a while was profitable but eventually the mine was closed, leaving it with a 360 foot shaft which would slowly fill with water. Many years later, in

1857, the wife of William Burgess died. Burgess was a heavy drinker, con man, thief, sheep stealer and a generally unpleasant fellow. His wife had died leaving him with three children, Tom and Emma who were old enough to be put into service at a farm at North Molton, and young Anna at just seven years old.

Burgess needed to be rid of Anna and took her to a house called South Hill in Withypool to ask James and Sarah Hayes to take her in. They declined, they already had a child of their own and another on the way. Burgess was enraged and determined to seek revenge. Some days later, South Hill was consumed in flames. Although James and Sarah Hayes escaped, James's sixty-three-year-old father along with Matthew and Grace Sharpland died in the flames. All three were buried in Simonsbath churchyard. Had Burgess taken revenge?

Burgess and Anna moved into lodgings at White Water Cott, conveniently near the White Water Inn. He paid the landlady for his own keep and half a crown a week for the keep of his daughter. The problem Burgess faced was that the little money he had barely covered the keep plus the high cost of his drinking habit. He needed to find another source of income. He went to the Reverend Thornton and told him how he had lost his horse and pig – a complete untruth. The vicar accepted his story and gave him a note which he could take to various well-to-do persons and plead for money from them.

Duped vicar turns detective

His pleas were met with understanding and the money arrived – but Burgess spent it all on drink. When the Reverend Thornton realised how he had been duped, he was furious and quietly determined that he would keep an eye on the behaviour of Burgess. As word went around of Burgess's dishonest intentions, so the charity dried up and Burgess again faced the quandary of how to feed his drink habit and pay for his daughter's keep. His never-to-be-forgiven solution was a cruel one. He decided to murder his own child.

In June 1857, he packed a bag with Anna's clothes and explained to his landlady, Mrs Marley, that he would be away for a couple of days while he took his daughter to her grandmother's in Porlock Weir. He then left with the child who would never be seen alive again. He took her up onto the moor and murdered her. Under cover of darkness, he buried her pitiful little body in a shallow grave. Unknowingly, he left a piece of her skirt protruding from the soil, in just the way that a sheep-stealer like himself would mark the shallow grave of a stolen sheep to be collected later.

Two villains walked the moor the following morning and spotted the piece of rag. Assuming it was a buried sheep, they left the grave alone but, on meeting Burgess passed comment on their discovery to check that it was Burgess's booty and not that of an intruder on his patch – honour amongst thieves. Burgess claimed it as one of his and thanked them for pointing it out. He realised that he had to move the body and this he did, again under cover of darkness, this time carrying her across the moor to the disused Wheal Eliza mine where, having stripped her of her clothes, he dropped her little body down the shaft, into the waters below, assuming that she was never to be found again. But he had not allowed for the inquisitive mind of the Reverend Thornton.

Around the back of the White Cottage Inn, the charred remains of what appeared to be a girl's dress was discovered. The Reverend Thornton was made aware of the discovery. He took the remains of the material to Mrs Marley who confirmed that it matched Anna's dress. Thornton now suspected that she had been murdered, and by her father. He sent William Court off to Porlock Weir with instructions that, without arousing any suspicions, he was to discover if Anna had ever reached her grandmother's house. On his return, he reported that Burgess had paid the grandmother a visit, but Anna was not with him. Although the evidence was only circumstantial, Thornton now had enough to convince him that the most heinous of crimes had been committed.

Thornton, now with the bull firmly by the horns, set the wheels of detection in motion. He sent the parish constable to Lynmouth where instinct told him that Burgess may have taken a ship to South Wales.

He then got William Court, who was a forester and knew the moors like the back of his hand, to organise a search party – looking for a grave. Meanwhile he set off for Curry Rivel, many miles away, on the other side of Taunton, where the chief constable lived, riding through the night to reach him. He arrived early in the morning, indeed the chief constable was still shaving. He convinced the police officer to return with him to Simonsbath where he was certain that there was a murder to be solved. Arriving later that day, they listened to the news that was coming back from the enquiries which Thornton had set in motion.

William Court reported that they had found a grave on the moor, a mile from the inn where the charred clothing was found. It was empty and could have been a body or a sheep. They had no way of knowing – but it was suspicious. Then the constable reported on his visit to Lynmouth. Yes, Burgess had been there and taken a boat to Swansea. The South Wales police were notified and they soon spotted the stranger with the broad Somerset accent. He was arrested, returned to Simonsbath, questioned by Thornton and then locked up in Dulverton Gaol. Although his pockets contained a pair of Anna's shoes, there was no proof of her murder. The months passed by with no fresh evidence and with Burgess admitting nothing. Without a body, no case of murder could be brought against Burgess. In time, everyone in the area knew the circumstances.

Now, while there is honour amongst thieves, not even criminals tolerate child murder. The two sheep stealers, who had unwittingly discovered Anna's first grave, realised that it must have been where Anna was buried. But they could hardly report their suspicions to the police. Sheep stealing was a hanging offence. They were, however, determined that the truth must out but not at risk of their own lives. They went to Thornton and, under a pledge of confidentiality, told the vicar what had happened in respect of Anna's first grave. Then came the breakthrough for which Thornton had been hoping. They continued by telling him that they had been on the moor one night, no need to ask what they were doing, when they saw what they assumed to be a stranger, carrying a load over his shoulder, which he threw down the mineshaft at the Wheal Eliza mine.

The case closes

Finally Thornton was close to having the evidence he needed to ensure Burgess was brought to justice. He notified the magistrates at Dulverton and the prolonged task of pumping out the mine was commenced. It took three months and then a young lad was winched down with a tarpaulin sack. When he came back to the surface, the sack was lowered to the ground. Thornton stepped forward and opened the sack. It contained the almost unrecognisable remains of poor little Anna. Her face had completely disappeared. Thornton ensured that she was given a Christian burial in the Simonsbath churchyard.

There was now sufficient evidence of a murder and Burgess confessed. He was later tried at Taunton, found guilty and sentenced to death. Thornton knew that Burgess's two older children had to be told what had happened, that their younger sister was dead, murdered by their own father. He took on the responsibility himself and was surprised by their reaction. It came as no surprise to them at all and they declined their father's request to see him one last time.

The Reverend Thornton visited Burgess prior to his execution. After shaking hands, Burgess admitted that he had killed his daughter simply because of the cost of his drink. He also confessed to burning the home of James Hayes, and causing the deaths of three other people. He was publicly hanged in January 1859.

Reverend Arthur Courtenay Jenoure

The Reverend Jenoure was one of Somerset's longest serving priests, serving at the Exmoor village of Cutcombe from 1923 until the mid 1960s when, in his '90s, he finally retired. In that long career, he quietly served his community but his voice was to be heard loud and clear across the nation in 1929 when he cried 'MURDER' from his parish pulpit.

Mollie Philips was seventeen years old and stood at a plump five foot three inches tall. She had grown up with her mother, sister and stepfather at Rocks Cottage. She worked at Rocks Farm, just a mile away, and it was from there that she left on her final journey. She was a sturdily-built young girl, noted for her cheerful nature and it was with a smile on her cheeks that she turned and waved goodbye to Annie Rawle, the housekeeper, as she shouted to her that she would be back in time to feed the chickens. It was a warm sunny day as she strode off, wearing a lightweight coat and a blue Tammy over her dark hair. She was heading for Cutcombe where she planned to visit her aunt but was never to arrive.

Mollie Philips disappears

The alarm was raised when she failed to return and her aunt declared that she had never arrived. A massive search was organised covering 50 square miles of Exmoor. A huge crowd of locals gathered at the Crown Hotel at Exford, dozens of them on horseback, scores of others on foot. Mineshafts were explored, a pond was drained, ditches dragged, moorland and woods thoroughly searched, but to no avail. The search was extended to the Brendon Hills and Luxborough – but still nothing. September turned to October, autumn turned to winter and the seasons passed, with no fresh news. Then fifteen months after her disappearance, as March approached its end, Jack Hawkins and Donald Grant, who farmed at Hawkington Farm, were crossing the 150-acre Codsend Moor when they made the horrific discovery. They had been burning rough grass to encourage new growth when Grant saw what were clearly human bones projecting from the ground, about 100 yards from the track which leads up to Dunkery Beacon. All that were visible was a skull and the ribs of one side of the body, the rest being submerged in the boggy ground where a spring bubbled up to the surface. Mollie Philips had finally been found but her release from the moor had to wait. There was insufficient daylight left and a lone police constable was left to guard the scene overnight, alone on a misty moor, with a partially-destroyed decomposing body.

In the morning, the recovery process began. It was spring and the ground was well-soaked from the winter's rain. It was impossible to reach the body without sinking into the bog. Before they could reach it, a trench had to be dug and filled in with solid matter in order to approach the site safely. The spot lay on a direct line between a hunting gate and a field gate. As the body was extracted, a 20-kilogram stone was found to be pressing against one side of Mollie's body, as if it had been placed there deliberately to sink her. The county pathologist, Dr Godfrey Carter, then joined the party. He raised questions about the nature of the bog. Whilst it was impassable in the spring, what was it like in September, at the end of a long dry spell? Opinions differed, some saying that they had driven cattle across it, others saying that it was always dangerous. There was a confusion of opinions.

At the post-mortem, it was revealed that there were no injuries as such. Her clothing and flesh were more or less intact where her body had remained submerged. Her coat and hat that she had been wearing when she left the farm were never found. At the inquest, the jury heard that the cause of death was possibly shock due to exposure, or maybe drowning. They were told how Codsend Moor was nowhere near any possible route that Mollie would have been taking that day. The coroner added that the position of her body suggested that she had fallen in, rather than being dumped, and gave his opinion that had a person been carrying her, then they would also have been taken down by the bog. He suggested that the heavy stone against her body had probably just arrived there under pressure from the spring water.

The jury, after half an hour's deliberation returned a verdict of 'death by misadventure when she was hurrying away in fright from someone'. It was a verdict which was not accepted by the people who knew Mollie Philips and who knew the moor. It was a verdict determined by the townsfolk of Minehead. Perhaps if a couple of Exmoor people had been included in the jury, the relevant questions would have been asked, and a different verdict determined. That was how the Reverend Jenoure felt. He was angry with the verdict and was about to let the world know.

'MURDER' from the pulpit

There was huge suspicion over the jury's verdict. Mollie had disappeared at the end of September, at the end of a long hot summer. Later that year, at the end of another dry spell, two local men entered the bog, one carrying the other, and nobody sank. This would suggest that Mollie could not have sunk in the bog at the time she disappeared but perhaps was carried there later. And what of the 20-kilogram stone. Could that not have been placed on her body to encourage it to sink in the bog and then have rolled off to one side as her body sank? At the inquest it appears to have gone unmentioned that the bog contained no boulders and that the stone appeared to have been taken from a bank many yards away. And Codsend Moor was nowhere near Mollie's route. Murder had to be considered and the vicar was determined that it should be.

At Mollie's funeral, over which Jenoure presided, he told the congregation, which included many press men, that overwhelmingly the local population knew it had to be murder. How could anyone believe that a strong young woman, who knew the moor like the back of her hand, would run into a bog, which probably didn't exist at the end of the dry spell, and fail to extricate herself? He declared that a jury of twelve-year-olds could have made a better job of it and to expect him and his parishioners to accept the verdict of misadventure was nothing less than an insult to their intelligence. How could four hotel owners, a plumber, a draper and a garage owner, all from Minehead understand the girl or the moor? The press grabbed his reaction for their headlines and linked it with the vicar's pledge that the villagers of ten parishes would sign a petition if asked to do so. The resultant publicity brought the case back to the boil. The police made further searches of the bog and discovered Mollie's spectacles and belt buckle.

The unsolved mystery of Mollie's death was even raised as a question in the House of Commons when the Home Secretary was asked if he was going to take any further action. As a result of this, the Attorney General called for a report from the Public Prosecutor, and the Public Prosecutor sent a detective to investigate at Cutcombe. With no new evidence, the Attorney General declared that the original verdict must stand. The Reverend Jenoure objected once again. He quoted a legal precedent from 1908 in which Justice Phillimore stated that an inconsistent verdict cannot stand. He argued that if Mollie Philips was running away in fright from someone at the time of her death, as the jury had decided was the case, then it could not be misadventure, but manslaughter at the very least. It had long been recognised that if an individual terrorised someone into an action which resulted in their death, then there is a case of manslaughter, if not murder, to be answered.

As far as the authorities were concerned, the case was officially closed, but the Reverend Jenoure declared otherwise. As far as he and the people of his parish were concerned, Mollie had been murdered and they still awaited the identification of her killer. None was ever found.

The vindictive vicar

Administering justice has never been easy, unless the perpetrator of a crime confesses the guilt. Otherwise, the accused remains innocent in the eyes of the law until proven guilty. This clearly acts as a barrier to justice especially in those trials where there is insufficient evidence to prove guilt beyond reasonable doubt. Imagine a trial where a young girl is brutally murdered. If the killer goes free, who knows when he may murder again. It is easy to understand how a police officer, in such cases, may allow evidence to be fabricated. His motive is to see justice done, not to corrupt the legal system per se. Take a situation where the accused has an alibi which removes him from the scene of the crime – but others contradict the alibi. Perhaps the police officer could be forgiven for not providing evidence of the alibi which he didn't believe.

In the case of the murder of Betty Trump, for which William Flood stood accused, it was the vicar, the Reverend Dr Palmer, who was acting as the chairman of the magistrates and ensured the relevant evidence failed to be presented, evidence which would prove the accused to be innocent.

Thirteen-year-old Betty Trump lived at Buckland St Mary, in the Blackdown Hills. For a year, she had been living with her grandmother, her family being at Winsham near Chard. In February 1823, the family were re-united when her parents also moved to Buckland. They had been together for just two weeks when Betty's parents asked her to go to Winsham, to her older sister's house, and ask if she could stay with her. At the same time her mother instructed her to make some purchases on her return journey, plates, a spoon, needles and thread. It was an 8-mile walk each way and Betty was told to return the same day if possible, otherwise on the following day at the latest. It was 20 February when she set off.

There was little concern when Betty failed to arrive home later that day, but concern set in when the following day passed with still no sign of the young girl. On the morning of the third day, a Saturday, another sister, Ann, was sent to Winsham to see if Betty was still with her older sister. It was then discovered that Betty had arrived safely on the first day and had left by three o'clock in the afternoon, heading for home, with the purchases still to be made.

When Ann arrived home with the news, her parents, Samuel and Elizabeth, began to search the route Betty would have followed and made enquiries along the way. They discovered that Betty had made the required purchases and had passed through Combe St Nicholas on her way home. A search party was organised the following morning and it was Daniel Parsons who discovered her body, with a slit throat, in Coppice Burrows, just 50 yards from the main road. Her basket lay at her side, apparently untouched.

The post-mortem examination revealed that her throat had been cut with a sharp knife or billhook. After the post-mortem, sightseers flocked in their hundreds to view the body, indeed so many were there that the funeral had to be delayed. Finally laid to rest, it was time to discover her killer.

Reports came in that two sailors had been seen in the vicinity of the crime at about the right time and it was the coroner's opinion that the nature of the injuries suggested that at least two people were involved. Unfortunately in the days that had passed since her murder, the two unknown sailors had disappeared forever.

Then a key witness came forward, William Flood. He stated how he had heard what sounded like a child shouting in the Coppice Burrows area one evening, but he couldn't remember which evening, and he assumed it was just a child being chastised in her own home and hence nothing to do with him. He had done himself no favours in offering this information. The coroner was not happy with such vague details and told Flood so. Then the rumours started. Perhaps Flood was the killer. He had been Betty's Sunday School teacher. Yes, that was true, but there was no truth in the rumour that Betty had pleaded with her mother not to make her go to Sunday school. There was no truth in the rumour that the police had found bloodstained, partially-burned clothing at Flood's house.

The fact that these rumours were totally unfounded was revealed publicly much later, but in the short-term were suppressed. The Reverend Dr Palmer, as a magistrate, accepted the rumours and a warrant for the arrest of William Flood was issued. When evidence was produced to contradict the rumours, he ignored it. Flood's home was searched and no incriminating evidence was found. Nonetheless, he was arrested and questioned by the vicar.

Because of the lack of solid evidence, the magistrates were obliged to release the prisoner but in order to ensure a conviction, the Reverend Palmer set up a committee of men who swore to carry out an investigation, revealing to no one other than themselves any of their findings. A £100 reward was offered for information leading to a conviction and a pardon offered to any accomplice who came forward, unless they took part in the actual killing. Even a Bow Street runner was allocated to the case.

Scores of people were interviewed and the evidence gathered in. William Flood remained the prime suspect and, with the power of hindsight, it is easy to understand how he stood unjustly accused. It was all a matter of timing and the problem of a clock which was always forty-five minutes fast. Various individuals gave evidence that they had seen young Betty Trump on her way home. All of the estimated timings made sense. One person said she saw her at 7.30, and another at 7.45, there being fifteen minutes walking time between the two sightings. It was all proving to be reliable.

Then William Flood gave his evidence as to where he had been and when. He stated how he had been muck spreading and had finished around half past five. He had then fed the cattle at Street Ash Farm, then headed for New House Farm having spoken to Honor Marsh on the way. He arrived at the farm at about a quarter past six. All of these people were prepared to confirm his movements, movements which would prove he could not have been at the place of the murder at the right time to be the killer.

However, our dubious vicar was determined to prove that Flood was guilty and made it almost impossible for him to prepare or offer any defence. Flood was allocated an attorney to help him, Mr. Cox from Honiton, but the Reverend Palmer denied him access to his client until the actual day of the trial.

Meanwhile, the vicar and his committee had produced another piece of damning evidence which defies belief. Philip Wyatt, a West Somerset carpenter and poet, was also a fortune teller. Although the magistrates would not allow Flood's attorney to visit his client, they granted the fortune teller access to the prisoner. Prior to his visit, Wyatt had been to Betty Trump's grave and allegedly spent the next three days and nights waiting for some communication from her. On the third night, he claimed, her spirit appeared and the ghost of Betty Trump named her murderer. Wyatt caught hold of Flood's hand, raised it in the air and declared 'This is your murderer'. Well done, vicar! That'll convince any jury.

In another dirty ploy, one of Palmer's secretive committee visited Flood and told him that there was now more than enough evidence to hang him, and it would probably be at Taunton in a few days – so perhaps he'd better prepare himself. In other words, confess and make his peace with his maker.

Eventually the case was presented to the magistrates. Various witnesses gave their evidence and a clear picture appeared as to exactly where Betty was and when during her final hours. Likewise a clear picture was being drawn as to the movements of William Flood. If he was where all the witnesses placed him at the times they stated, he could not have had time to murder the young girl. But there was one flaw in the evidence. His movements up to just before the time of the killing were accepted. Then the blacksmith and his apprentice had stated that they had seen William Flood pass the forge as the forge clock struck eight o'clock. This created a forty-five-minute gap during which Flood would be unable to account for his movements and clearly provided sufficient time to perpetrate the murder. However, it had been known for years that the forge clock was forty-five minutes fast, and making that adjustment would remove the unaccounted time. The Reverend Palmer refused to allow that explanation to be presented. Nor did he allow other witnesses to present their evidence that would confirm his movements at the time of the murder and thereafter. Their evidence would have accounted perfectly for his complete movements during the hours around the time of the murder. Again, the vicar declined to allow the evidence to be presented since, as he explained, it would only contradict previously heard evidence and that would serve no useful purpose at all!

Mr Cox, Flood's attorney, pleaded for the opportunity to present the vital witnesses, and to put the blacksmith in the witness box to provide the evidence that the clock was always forty-five minutes fast. In his summing up, the chairman of the magistrates emphasised that it was the forty-five minutes for which Flood could not account that proved his guilt. Again, Mr Cox interrupted, stating he still had seven witnesses to produce.

After the shambles of his trial, Flood was taken to Ilchester Gaol pending the Summer Assizes. Brought to trial there, the judge found it hard to believe that the prisoner should ever have been brought before him. There was clearly no evidence that he had any part in the murder of Betty Trump. The Reverend Dr Palmer, playing unsuccessfully at amateur sleuth, had ignored vital evidence and had allowed himself to become blinkered to one theory and one theory alone. No doubt Flood's attorney walked out of the court muttering 'Blame it on the Vicar!'

8

Treachery, Treason and Torture

Smuggling and wrecking vicars

Vicars and the Ten Commandments don't always go hand in hand. We have seen in earlier chapters that at least adultery is on the crime sheet, but nowhere in the Ten Commandments does smuggling or fraud get a mention. Perhaps that is how the vicar of Otterhampton, near Combwich, cleared his conscience when in 1380 he was found guilty of smuggling wine and other goods into the country.

Even earlier, in the twelfth century, there appears to be a blatant case of fraud in which no less than an abbot was involved. Somewhere around 1250, Abbot Henry de Blois was on a visit to Somerset, inspecting properties belonging to the church at Brent Knoll. He spotted a particularly bountiful piece of land on which was growing a fine crop of corn, so good that it immediately caught the eye. He asked the owner of the land by what name the property was known. 'No value' was the reply and it was explained how the land had been given by an earlier abbot, Abbot Herlewin, to a local knight. Naturally Abbot Henry's suspicions were aroused and he went to check the abbey records. Sure enough, there were the details of the transfer of the land, described as having no value and

Henry de Blois

nor would it ever have any value. The knight was granted permission to harvest his wheat crop and thereafter. Abbot Henry reclaimed the property. Presumably the gift had been a back-hander for favours granted.

But back to smuggling. If a ship is wrecked and the goods are swept ashore, then it was the custom that the nearby villagers would race down to the shore to collect the spoils, always on a first come, first served basis. Hence it was vital to be at the front of the queue. There is a tale of another parson who benefited from such trade, especially at the expense of others. On one occasion, the parson was delivering his sermon from the pulpit, when a messenger entered the church, walked up to the pulpit and passed a written message to the parson. The parson studied the message as he continued delivering his sermon, without interruption. The message told how a ship was breaking up in the nearby bay. He continued with the sermon as he stepped down from the pulpit, removing his clerical robes as he walked towards the door of the church, and there, like a greyhound straining in the trap, he delivered the end of the sermon and the blessing. With that, standing in the doorway, so as to bar anyone else's exit, he announced the news that there was a wreck in the bay and shouted 'Let's all start fair!' as he sprinted off with the benefit of a huge head start.

The murderous vicar

The wealthy squire of Chelvey was badly injured in an accident and was most grateful when he was rescued by a parson called Hibbetson. The parson nursed the squire back to health and the two became such close friends that the squire altered his will in favour of the parson. It was the biggest mistake of his life. Having been rescued and nursed by the parson, the parson then murdered him for his inheritance. Hibbetson was never punished for his crime but later died in a great thunderstorm on Exmoor.

The conman and the Bible class

It was 1894 and Massa Johnson had arrived in the seaside town of Weston-super-Mare. He was a tailor by trade and had joined a Bible class at a local church. He soon proved himself to be very popular, mostly thanks to his silver tongue, and was playing a leading role in the group. It was time to instigate the sting.

He quietly dropped subtle hints that he had unexpectedly inherited a fortune. As a good Christian, it was his intention to use at least part of the inheritance to establish a young men's home and towards that end he opened up negotiations to purchase a town property which was becoming available. Naturally his fellow Bible class members were full of admiration and basked in the reflected glory. However, he explained, until the inheritance transactions were complete, he was temporarily short of funds and it would be a shame to miss the opportunity to purchase the premises. If only he could find a way of raising the cash in the short term!

It wasn't long before the offers to lend money were coming in. He even promised to repay those who helped not just by refunding their cash, but also to take them on a Mediterranean holiday and actually went to one young man's employer to plead with him to let his employee have sufficient time off from work to permit the trip. £15 here, £20 there, the money rolled in. The Bible class even held a prayer meeting to pray for yet more cash. The outcome was predictable. He disappeared, taking with him their dreams of a young men's home and all of their hard-earned cash. An anonymous letter to the *Weston-Super-Mare Gazette* pointed out that whilst expressing sympathy for those robbed by this conman, it was their own greed which had placed them in that vulnerable position.

Robert Parsons – Gunpowder Plot conspirator?

Remember, remember, the fifth of November;
gunpowder, treason and plot.

Was a Somerset priest involved in the Gunpowder Plot? Almost certainly, but he kept well away from the action.

Robert Parsons was a Jesuit priest born in June 1546, the son of a Nether Stowey blacksmith, the middlemost of eleven children. He was raised as a Catholic and educated at Stogursey, Taunton and Balliol College, Oxford. In July 1575 he joined the Society of Jesus and became a missionary four years later. He followed a life of mystery and intrigue, plotting and scheming against the Protestant authorities. In June 1579 he landed at Dover, disguised as a soldier, and thereafter followed an intense period of espionage. He was continually and unsuccessfully hunted by government agents who were unable to capture this elusive 'Pimpernel' character. As part of his cover, he used a number of aliases including that of Robert Cowbuck.

Much of his time was spent travelling around Europe, drumming up support and raising finances for the Spanish Armada. It is therefore quite possible, though with no proof of such, that he would have influenced the plans for the Gunpowder Plot. So where does the evidence come from? We know that from 1580 onwards, he was responsible for the Catholic Church's English mission, which he ran at great risk to himself. He kept a printing press in England but when it became too risky, he moved it to Belgium, where he served as rector at Douai, and there started a campaign to organise the armed intervention on behalf of the English Catholics.

Parsons was never held to account for any of his espionage activities, albeit one of his closest friends was executed for his part in the Gunpowder Plot, and Parsons certainly kept a low profile in the period following the capture of Guy Fawkes. It is alleged that he obtained the hangman's rope used for his friend's execution and kept it until his death as a reminder, or perhaps as a penance. He was a close associate of Cardinal William Allen and together they plotted against the Protestant English monarchs, favouring an armed invasion by the continental Catholics. He died in April 1610 in Rome where he was serving the Pope as rector of the English Church. No one will ever know if he was involved in any way with the Gunpowder Plot but suffice it to say that he was always in the right places at the right time.

Reverend Edmund Peachum

Treason was a lively issue throughout the seventeenth century. Enemies abroad (France and Spain) and enemies at home (Catholics and Puritans) were a constant threat to the monarchy. James l lived in perpetual fear of treachery and his spies were ever vigilant to a careless phrase or a suggestive comment which may have hinted at a possible threat to himself.

The Reverend Edmund Peachum was a Somerset clergyman who fell foul of the resultant witch hunt which was born from the constant fear of rebellion. He had written certain articles which when discovered were considered to be treasonous. There was an ambiguity to them. He was clearly concerned about the stability of the country and questioned what could happen if, for example, the king died. The king and his protectors, however, interpreted his writing to be a suggestion that the king should die. He was adamant that he was innocent of such thoughts. They were equally adamant that he was guilty. In a king-versus-priest battle, the king normally wins.

What was it that was so contentious in his writings?

The people might rise in rebellion against these taxes.

All the king's officers might be put to the sword.

When Prince Charles assumed the throne, might not the people say 'Come, this is the heir, let us kill him.'

On a sudden, the King might be strucken with death,
perhaps within eight days

These were clearly questions not statements – but were they a conspiracy to murder? His writings were never voiced from the pulpit, nor were they ever published. They were simply discovered in his study and they were enough to get him arrested. The king was concerned that Peachum may have been aware of a plot to overthrow him. Consequently he ordered his team of interrogators to torture Peachum to discover the truth. In January 1615, Peachum was interrogated in the Tower of London.

Peachum this day was examined before torture, in torture, between tortures,
and after torture; notwithstanding, nothing could be drawn from him.

We can assume that the torture was in the extreme. Peachum was asked to identify who had advised him on the plot; who else was aware of the plot; what did he intend to do with his writings; and what made him write that the king might be killed in eight days. The questions, clearly indicating a king in fear of his life, were asked over and over again. Each time, despite the severity of the torture, Peachum's answers were the same. No amount of torture could draw out any other response. Despite there being no real evidence against him, he was found guilty and sentenced to death. Before he had chance to attend his execution, he died in prison in Taunton, the victim of the severe torture which he had endured.

Bishop from Bawdrip hanged for sodomy

John Atherton was born in 1598 at Bawdrip, the son of the local rector. Always a controversial character, he proved to be the cause of concern for both parents. On one occasion, as a young lad, when out riding with his mother, he stopped and stared at a gallows. It fascinated the young man with thoughts of how it would be to hang there himself. 'I'll hang myself from there one day, mother. With my horses bridle. That's how I'll do it.' said John to his mother.

The impact was devastating. The previously calm mother, enjoying a morning's ride, was now quite distraught. To hear her son talk this way terrified her. Surely he couldn't mean what he said. Surely it was just a young man's fantasy. John's father, on hearing how his son had behaved, was furious. How could the boy upset his mother so? 'It will be a truly short life for you, my lad, if that's the way you behave. How dare you show such disrespect to your mother'. Perhaps unbeknown to himself, he had predicted his own premature end.

At the age of sixteen, John was sent to Gloucester Hall to further his education taking a bachelor's degree before transferring to Lincoln College to complete his Masters. Full-time education complete, he entered Holy Orders and became rector of Huish Champflower in Somerset. He continued his learning and developed an in-depth understanding of ecclesiastical law and attracted the attention of Thomas Wentworth who was the Earl of Strafford and Lord Lieutenant of Ireland. It was through this association that John was appointed the Prebendary of St John's, Dublin on 22 April, 1630. In 1635 he became the Chancellor of Christ Church and on 4 May, 1636 took the position of Bishop of Waterford and Lismore, a position in which he was described as having 'behaved himself for some time with great prudence, though forward enough, if not too much, against the Roman Catholics'.

His unpopularity appears to stem from his attempts to acquire large areas of land for the Church. One particular claim was against the Earl of Cork and in this way he made himself many powerful enemies and hastened his own premature downfall. In 1640 he was accused of 'unnatural crime' and found guilty of sodomy with his tithe proctor. Throughout the case he pleaded his innocence in the face of flimsy evidence. His sole accuser was a man lacking integrity and credibility. It was his word against Atherton's. The accuser won the day and the outcome was inevitable. With John out of the way, the threatened loss of lands would come to an end.

The trial over, John Atherton was condemned to death by hanging and taken to Dublin Gaol awaiting execution. One contemporary said John 'fell a sacrifice to that litigation rather than justice'. Right to the end, John maintained his absolute innocence. On his execution day, he read a service to his fellow prisoners, dignified to the last, and proceeded to the gallows with the execution party.

A huge crowd gathered for what was clearly a popular occasion and gave John the opportunity to address the public and protest his innocence. Alas his statement and final prayers were subjected to the barracking of a local hooligan who had climbed the gallows and, enjoying his five minutes of attention, threw verbal abuse at the condemned bishop. It was an undignified end on that winter's day on 5 December, 1640.

Years later, the man on whose sole evidence John was condemned, was himself brought to justice and hanged. At the gallows, he confessed his sins and in that confession declared that the accusation he made against John Atherton had been completely false. John Atherton was innocent, the victim of an immoral Earl of Cork.

An illustrated report from 1641 of John Atherton's execution

9
Unpopular Vicars

In fairness, the majority of vicars are popular fellows, well respected within their parish, frequently at the very centre, acting as the glue which holds an otherwise disparate group of individuals together as a community. They are the shoulder to lean on, the father figure, the guide and mentor, the trusted confidant. But, just now and again a parish ends up with a vicar that they wish would attach himself to a different parish.

What makes a vicar unpopular? A holier than thou attitude, pointing the accusing finger at sinners? Maybe a vicar who runs off with someone else's wife. Or perhaps a vicar who has gained too much control and in a mafia-style coup needs to be taken down a peg or two, as was the case in Bridgwater in 1381.

St Mary's versus St John's

Bridgwater's first church, dating back to Celtic times, was the church of St Mary the Virgin. Around 1220, an Augustinian priory, St John's, was built to serve the needs of pilgrims and the poor or infirm, but definitely not lepers, lunatics, epileptics, pregnant or breast-feeding mothers, anyone with contagious diseases nor the wealthy. But it did care for the education of the poor lads of the town.

It was a self-governing establishment with its master being elected from within its own brethren. Part of their role was to provide someone to serve the church of St Marys and another to serve on a daily basis at the services in the castle chapel. So that was how it began. St John's served St Mary's, not the other way round. As the decades passed, the establishment at St John's grew in size and influence. It was even granted control of the churches of St Mary's in Bridgwater, St George's in Wembdon in 1284, Northover, Isle Brewers, Chilton, Edstcok and others as far afield as Cornwall. Indeed, it became so powerful that in 1300 the master was summoned to perform military service against the Scots.

In 1380, Thomas, the master of St John's, complained that a number of local tradesmen had attacked the hospital, vandalising the building, beating up the servants and stealing what they could. It was a rebellion against the power which the prior at St John's had acquired. He loaned money, held deeds to properties against those loans, and then forced the borrowers into a corner. They even collected tithes from St Mary's. This caused great bitterness between the two establishments, St Mary's having lost all effective control to the new boys at St John's.

The following year saw similar unrest across the country which developed into the Wat Tyler Rebellion. The rebellion was crushed and Wat Tyler executed. In York, Scarborough and Bridgwater, the news had failed to get through and the troubles continued. Nicolas Frompton, a priest who served St Mary's, had seen the way the Knights of St John had been treated in London and he planned to do the same in Bridgwater with the opposition at St John's. He recruited Thomas Engilby, a yeoman, who raised a mob of 14 men. They forced their way into the house of the Knights of St John and seized William Camel, the master, demanding that he transfer all properties and rights to Frompton. In addition they burned a large number of deeds and bonds and bullied the master into signing a £200 ransom promise. Finished at the priory, they moved on to Sydenham Manor, burning more deeds. Then they burned the house and goods of Walter Baron of East Chilton. Worst still, they had Walter Baron beheaded.

On the Friday, Frompton headed towards Ilchester Gaol, forcing John Bursy of Long Sutton to go with him. At Ilchester they removed Hugh Lavenham from the gaol and made John Bursy behead him in order that they could take the head on a spear back to Bridgwater. There it was displayed on the town bridge alongside that of Walter Baron.

All of this was done in the name of St Mary's. But then they heard the news that elsewhere the Wat Tyler rebellion had been crushed several days before. Engilby fled the country and, in his absence, was condemned to death. Before the month was out he was pardoned and Frompton meanwhile had disappeared, never to be heard from again. Now, that is what can happen when a vicar, or prior in this case, becomes too unpopular.

Many years later, and again in Bridgwater, an unpopular member of the clergy suffered once again from a hostile crowd. That man was the Methodist Reverend Whitfield.

The Methodist Movement

Methodism began in the 1730s when John and Charles Wesley were at Oxford as Anglican clergymen. They were influenced by German Protestant refugees known as Moravians and were converted to that movement. At the university they formed the Holy Club and in so doing introduced structure to their religion, with time-tables. This earned them the name of Methodists. George Whitfield was one of their early followers and all three were to visit Somerset on a regular basis, filling what appeared to be a religious vacuum which existed at the time. Local people had lost interest in the Anglican Church and were looking for an alternative.

We can only imagine the anger felt by the Anglicans as members of their congregations flocked to this new religious group. In the beginning, they were welcomed as clergymen who were reviving an interest in religion, but then they became resented. When the use of a local pulpit was refused, the Methodists would preach in the open air and eventually broke away from the established Church. George Whitfield was the first Methodist to preach in Somerset when he visited Keynsham and Publow in 1739. Later that same year, John Wesley preached in Bath and Pensford. On his third visit to Bath, Beau Nash challenged Wesley's right to preach there, and on his next visit, he was told by the sheriff that he was banned – but it didn't stop him preaching in the city at least 70 times. Wesley's preaching sessions were often opposed by the Anglican clergymen who in 1742 organised a hostile mob to disrupt the service. His visits to Shepton Mallet in 1746 and 1748 both resulted in riots. Fights broke out at Frome in 1751 and at Castle Cary a preacher was thrown into the duck pond. Nevertheless, he visited the county almost every year from 1730 to his death in 1791.

Water-cannoned out of the pulpit

John Wesley first visited Bridgwater in 1746 when he preached late on a September afternoon, and appeared regularly thereafter until 1749. When he re-appeared in 1760, on a miserably wet day, he described the town as 'a dead and uncomfortable place at best'. It has always amazed me that having made such a derogatory comment about the town, there were still sufficient followers to open two Wesleyan chapels.

However, still at Bridgwater, when George Whitfield took to the pulpit, so incensed were the local Anglicans that they arranged for the fire brigade to turn their hoses on him and blast him from the pulpit. With

George Whitfield

such hostile receptions, it is a wonder that the Wesleys kept returning. Indeed they didn't seem to like any of the Somerset locals. Wesley described the people of Wincanton as having 'just as much feeling as the benches they sit on'. The people of Fivehead were 'stupid people to deal with'. Frome folk were keen to listen but 'how little they profit from the listening' and he was surprised that any good could be done at 'poor, dead, quarrelsome Frome'.

Stogumber folk were similarly the recipients of clerical criticism. In 1629, John Streete, who was a Stogumber churchwarden, commented to the Bishop of Bath and Wells, on one of his visits to Taunton, that 'the parish of Stogumber is such a place as he never put his foot in the like, and that it is as odious a place to him as hell itself.' He continued by claiming that his three predecessors were all perjurers. A one-time vicar of Kingston St Mary had an equally low opinion of his parishioners when he quoted 'Monkton for the rich, Cheddon for the poor, Kingston for the thieves...!'

In 1718, John Yard made himself so unpopular at St Mary Magdalene church in Taunton, that he narrowly escaped being burnt alive in the market place. He had persuaded the church to erect a new pulpit with a magnificent canopy. The problem arose when it was realised that such a large and heavy structure would need a deeper foundation. The result of the subsequent excavation was that one of the main pillars of the church collapsed. That weakened the rest of the church structure and three more pillars collapsed bringing down a complete bay. In a matter of days the cost had escalated from £100 to £500.

Blood and guts in the pulpit

Who would have thought that the peaceful village of Leigh-on-Mendip could harbour such hatred against the local vicar? But he was hated and the anger boiled over in a most obnoxious way.

In the spring of 1854 the Reverend George Augustus Mahon took up his new post as the vicar of the church of St Giles at Leigh-on-Mendip. He soon formed the opinion that the village was full of drunks and consequently visited the local pub, the Tadhill Inn, at closing time. There, as the drinkers left the premises, he tackled them one by one, pouring scorn on them. He was particularly outspoken against Joseph Ashman, a local farmer, because Ashman was quite happy to give as good as he got. At a village revel, Ashman retaliated by leading a man dressed as a woman to the Reverend Mahon's front door, muttered anti-religious sentiments (presumably along the lines of 'stuff the vicar and stuff the Church!') and even muttered 'damn' a number of times, each of which was recorded by the rector to be produced later as evidence. Some days after, Ashman was at the top of a ladder as the rector passed by below. Ashman commented that 'Yer, I be up Jacob's Ladder, vicar.' Mahon was not amused.

The reverend gentleman took his complaint about Ashman's behaviour, including an accusation that the man was beating his wife, to the Reverend Horner who was not only the rector at nearby Mells, but also the lord of the manor and as such was the owner of many of the village's rented properties, including Ashman's farm.

In complaining to Horner, the Reverend Mahon brought to his neighbour's attention the amount of drinking that Joseph Ashman was doing, and coupled that with rumours that he was also beating his wife. The outcome of this complaint was that the Reverend Horner evicted Ashman from his farm, leaving him and his labourers unemployed. It was not a good way for the vicar to win the hearts and minds of this small tight-knit community.

Ashman's reaction was to seek revenge. It was a dark and wet Sunday evening, in September 1857. The lamps were lit in the church as the vicar took divine service. The congregation listened intently. Outside, Ashman had taken a gun and loaded it with blood and gore. He stealthily approached the church in the darkness, staying close to a wall for cover. Reaching the church he positioned himself outside of a window, took aim through the window and pulled the trigger. With an enormous bang which echoed around the church, the glass, blood and gore flew straight at the pulpit and engulfed the vicar mid-sermon.

Some of the congregation fled in panic. Others rushed forward to where the vicar stood dazed in the blood-covered pulpit, convinced that he was seriously wounded. It was soon realised that apart from some bruising and an eye injury caused by flying glass, he was reasonably OK. The blood was clearly not his. The rector immediately suspected Ashman and, having gone home to clean up, he instructed the village constable to arrest the suspect who was found, needless to say, at the Tadhill Inn, with two of his friends. All three were arrested and taken to Frome, but the two friends were later released. A detective was brought down from London to investigate a possible attempted murder, but there was no evidence to suggest murder was the intent, and so it was left as a local matter.

Ashman went to trial twice. The first time there appeared to be a reluctance to come forward from the various witnesses. Eventually, amidst a mass of conflicting evidence, Ashman was found guilty of unlawfully inflicting bodily harm and was sentenced to twelve months. The Reverend Mahon pleaded for clemency, not unreasonably since the judge had already pointed out to him that having Ashman evicted had invited the retaliation, and he considered that eviction was excessive punishment for basically doing no more than taking the Mickey out of the vicar. Subsequently the Reverend Mahon took a more diplomatic approach with his parishioners and over his remaining years won their hearts and minds.

The vicar who boiled over

Another unpopular vicar was the Reverend Trat of Old Cleeve near Watchet. It was 1604 and the incumbent rector of Old Cleeve was the Reverend Edward Brickenden. He had a life-time entitlement to the position and was also entitled to pass it on to an heir if he decided to do so. It was always understood that it would pass to Peter Smethwicke, his grandson. But fate steered a different course when the vicar recruited the Reverend Trat as his curate. Trat was a zealot who put the fear of God into the parishioners, threatening them with hellfire and damnation. From the pulpit, he terrorised them. One by one, the village turned against him and his congregation diminished. The hostility towards the new curate coincided with the discovery by

Peter Smethwicke that his grandfather, the Reverend Brickenden, was to pass the rectorship and the perpetual patronage of Old Cleeve to his new curate, the Reverend Trat. Smethwicke was furious and was at the forefront of a campaign of character assassination aimed at Trat. When Trat's wife drowned in an accident at Blue Anchor Bay, the disaster appeared to be heaven sent. It was soon agreed, by general consensus, that Trat must have schemed to ensure her presence in a position where she would be cut off by the tide. But nothing could be proven. Smethwicke and his friends agreed that they should take matters into their own hands.

The Reverend Trat wore a very distinctive hat and cloak and in this fashion travelled around the parish and neighbouring villages. He was easily recognisable simply from his profile as he travelled across the hills. To bring discredit on Trat, one of Smethwicke's friends dressed up in the style of the curate and then assaulted women in the woods. But that didn't work – the magistrate was not prepared to prosecute on the strength of similarity of dress.

Peter Smethwicke came up with a scheme and included Cyril Austen, Andrew Baker and Alice Walker in his plans. They hijacked the curate as he rode over the hills, dragged him from his horse and stabbed him to death. But they had to dispose of the body and here the plot thickened.

They took his body to his own home, removed his head and four limbs. The head was then cremated until it was unrecognisable. The body was put into a large container where Alice boiled the contents. The head was disposed of but the pot and its contents left in his house to create the illusion that Trat himself had boiled someone else's body and had then fled the village. To complete the illusion, Smethwicke's father dressed up as the curate and rode through the village ensuring sufficient witnesses saw the 'curate' leaving town.

Eventually Trat's disappearance drew the required attention. The alarm was raised and the police broke into his home to discover the gruesome remains of an unrecognisable body. The rumours immediately spread throughout the community that Trat had killed someone and left parts of their body in his house before disappearing. Smethwicke and his gang confirmed having seen the curate riding out of the village, wearing his distinctive hat and cape. It nearly worked but the astute village policeman spotted Trat's actual hat and cape behind the front door of his house. He soon realised that those who claimed to have seen him must have perpetrated the attempted illusion. In time all four villains came under arrest and were delivered up for trial, found guilty and hanged at the Stonegallows just outside of Taunton.

Difficult congregations

Whilst Trat's pulpit style appears to have driven his congregation away, imagine the disappointment a new vicar would get if he had no congregation at all, and it was Good Friday! That is exactly what happened to a new vicar at one Exmoor village. He had been in the village the best part of month and all seemed to be going well. He had been received by the residents of the village in a most friendly and welcoming manner, and since his arrival, the congregation had been picking up as each week passed. And then, out of the blue, there he was in the pulpit on Good Friday looking at mostly empty pews with just a few frail, hard-of-hearing ladies awaiting his delivery.

You can imagine the disappointment and his concern as to what he could possibly have done to offend his flock to such an extent that they organised a mass boycott. It was a huge anti-climax after such a good start in the village. With the service over, he approached the old ladies, convinced that they would inform him of whatever his mistake had been, in the sincere hope that he could recover the situation. They stared at him in amazement as if he were from a different planet, and in a way he was. Not being an Exmoor man, he was totally unaware of the local superstition that you should always plant your beans on Good Friday!

The same vicar was soon to realise the inconvenience of another local practice. In many Exmoor and Quantock villages, there is a tradition for the local children to tie the church gates at a wedding. Then as the married couple leave, the groom gives the children money or presents, and they cut the ribbon, releasing the newly married pair. However, at the vicar's new church, no one told him of another custom at weddings. Whilst the marriage service takes place at one end of the nave, at the other is the bell tower. It was the custom that one of the bell ringers would observe the service through a narrow window between the belfry and the nave. As the observer spotted the ring being slipped on the bride's finger, he would signal to the ringers who would then let loose with a massive and deafening peal of bells. The unfortunate new vicar, unaware of this practice, then had to complete the service over the deafening noise.

Another vicar whose sermon was noisier than usual was the rector of Wookey in 1906. He was reading the first lesson:

Did ever people hear the voice of God speaking out of the midst of the fire as thou hast heard, and live? Out of Heaven He made thee to hear His voice and upon the earth He showed thee His great fire.

Bang on cue, there was a thunderous crash as lightening struck a pinnacle on the church tower, splitting it in two. Roof timbers crashed down inside the church and the congregation rushed for the doors in a state of panic, convinced that the Lord had struck with anger. The only casualty was a swift which had been nesting on a beam and had been crushed by the tenor bell. At least no one fell asleep in during the sermon.

Sleeping congregations

In stark contrast, the congregation at Langford Budville around 1794 had a much quieter time. At one Sunday service, the vicar had droned on so long that the entire congregation were nodding off. One old man who had fallen asleep was dreaming that he was at a cock-fighting contest when during a quiet moment of prayer, from deep within his dream, he shouted aloud 'A shilling upon the red cock!' With that someone gave him a nudge hard enough to wake the dead and from then to his dying day he was known as 'The Red Cock'.

It was not the first time that he had been the brunt of local humour. In his earlier years, he had served as the church clerk and would often do the bible reading. He was overheard practising the reading one day. After he left, a local man crept up to the lectern and stuck a piece of paper onto the page such that the word 'tree' was replaced by 'horse'. At the Sunday service, the clerk read 'And they shall flourish like a young bay horse. Horse? It should not be horse! But by the Lord it is horse.'

Joseph Lee, who was the clerk and sexton of Broomfield church in the mid-1900s was another who had problems with the words from the bible readings, especially long words. He really struggled with Shadrach, Meschach and Abednego and found that he became completely tongue-tied. He overcame the problem by referring to these biblical characters as 'those chaps with the long names'.

It appears that the vicar at Wiveliscombe was as boring as his colleague at Langford Budville. In 1712 the church bought a bell and paid a man five shillings a year to ring it during the vicar's sermons whenever his congregation began to fall asleep. It was worse at Henstridge where the church sexton was paid to walk up and down the aisles not only with a bell but with a whip! Two years later the sexton was sacked for being drunk too often. He had failed to keep the church clean, failed to ring the bell before services and failed to weed the church grounds. Perhaps the straw that broke the camel's back was when he rang the bell so hard, that it broke free and smashed the bell wheel.

Robert Southey, the poet and close friend to Coleridge and Wordsworth, was once a young pupil at Mr Flower's school at Corston in North Somerset. He well remembered how the local vicar's sermon would drive him to sleep and many years later described it in verse:

I saw the church where I had slept away
The tedious service on a summer's day;
Or listening sad to all the preacher told
In winter waked and shivered in the cold.

He had clearly not enjoyed the experience.

In 1765, the clerk at Babcary church failed to turn up on Easter Sunday. He had sat drinking throughout the previous night and was unable to surface in the morning. This earned him a severe lecture from Parson Woodforde later that day but was then reconciled when he was invited to dinner at the parsonage. Now Parson James Woodforde was very fond of food and drink. He recorded in his diary how at one dinner for just 15 persons, they consumed between them 45 lbs of beef, a ham, six fowls, a roast saddle of mutton and two very rich puddings. He was by no means a bigot but recorded how he was surprised that a Roman Catholic he met appeared to be quite sensible, and a Non-conformist minister was apparently quite well behaved.

Bishops, archbishops and cardinals

A visit to the church at Brent Knoll will reveal some fascinating bench-end carvings. The ones of most interest are a series of three, the first showing a fox wearing a bishop's mitre, the next depicting his downfall and the third showing him hanging by the neck. The fox is possibly the representation of the Abbot of Glastonbury who made himself unpopular with the villagers of Brent Knoll when he claimed excessive tithes from them. Alternatively, and far more likely, it is the depiction of Richard Fox, the Bishop of Bath and Wells, who was equally unpopular. And so a local craftsman created the satirical bench ends in which the bishop is depicted as a fox, complete with mitre and crosier.

In the first scene, he is surrounded by his minions who have the heads of monkeys and who can be seen to be dominating the other animals and birds. The second carving is in two parts, almost like a cartoon strip. In the upper part, the fox has been stripped of his vestments and has been pinioned in foot cuffs. Birds and animals look on, one being the wise old owl, perhaps depicting a judge and jury. In the lower panel, the fox is in the stocks, presumably awaiting execution. The third and final panel shows the fox has been hanged and five geese have acted as executioners. Beneath the hanging fox, hounds are waiting for the body to be cut down, providing their supper.

Just what Richard Fox did to make himself so unpopular is unclear. What is certain is that the wishes of the parishioners to ridicule the bishop have been immortalised. Ridiculing bishops can be a dangerous occupation, but more dangerous by far is ridiculing a cardinal, as Sir Amyas Poulett was to discover.

Amyas Poulett was the High Sheriff of Somerset and as such was responsible for law and order. From the early days of the thirteenth century, the village of Lopen had an annual fair where there was plenty to eat and drink, and with entertainment such as bear-baiting, wrestling and cudgelling, a competition in which men attempt to club each other into a state of unconsciousness. One day, at the fair, a young student was proving to be a little too boisterous and so Sir Amyass had him locked in the stocks for disorderly conduct. The bright young student was Thomas Wolsey who at the time was employed by the Earl of Dorset to educate his sons. He was the humble son of a humble butcher but he was bright. He graduated from Oxford aged fifteen, destined to become the Archbishop of York, Cardinal of Rome, and Chancellor of England. Having achieved such high status, he remembered his adversary down in Somerset, the man who had him locked in the stocks, and had Sir Amyas placed under virtual house arrest for more than six years.

Sacked and reinstated

You have been warned. Avoid upsetting bishops and cardinals unless you are prepared to face the consequences. One vicar who fell foul of the Bishop of Bath and Wells was Richard de Rokebere in 1338. Richard was the vicar at Kingston St Mary and as far as he knew was making a good job of it. But then the Archdeacon of Taunton received a surprising communication declaring that Richard de Rokebere was 'pretending to be the vicar of Kyngstonne' and that henceforth no revenues were to be paid to him. The archdeacon swiftly made his way to Kingston where he read the bishop's letter aloud to the congregation. Richard was furious and told the archdeacon and his escorts to leave, declaring that 'If the bishop excommunicates me, I excommunicate him'. Then putting on his clerical garb, he celebrated mass, the archdeacon and his escort being locked outside so as not to witness the service within.

The archdeacon hastened off to find a constable and Richard de Rokebere was imprisoned and a substitute priest put in his place. However, it all turned out to be some sort of clerical error and Richard was re-instated on the instructions of the Court of Canterbury.

A hat trick of unsuitable rectors

For a village to have one bad vicar is unfortunate. To have two unsuitable vicars approaches carelessness – but three in a row! The village of Wambrook, close to the Dorset border, was such a village. From 1555 to 1591 their rector was John Marraker who was frequently incoherent and too familiar with his female parishioners. He was followed by Christopher Marraker who was rector from 1591 to 1621. Although he was a man of great learning, indeed he was tutor to Sir Simon D'Ewes and a recognised antiquarian writer, he was not appreciated by his parishioners who described him as having no regard for the souls of his scholars.

Then came Gamaliel Chase, from 1621 to 1645, who made it a hat trick of rectorial failures. He was thrown into prison, not once but twice, first by the Parliamentarians and then by the Royalists. Clearly he wasn't as astute as his predecessor, having a complete inability to chose the winning side.

Wrecked rectors

During the 1660s, Humphrey Blake was the vicar of Over Stowey. In 1670, he failed to take the pre-Christmas Sunday service, having drunk too much beer or wine the previous day. He was apparently quite well known for regularly swearing and for playing cards in the pubs in nearby Nether Stowey. A contemporary of Blake, Gratiosus Franklyn was the rector of Nunney and was well known for advising his congregation to drink the communion wine very sparingly on the rare occasion that he took communion. He apparently preferred to drink it all himself and was often so drunk that his clerk would have to find the Parson's place in the prayer book.

Reverend John Skinner of Camerton

In 1822, the Reverend John Skinner began to write his diary which provides wonderful detail of life in old Somerset, the mining village of Camerton in particular. Village life there came as quite a shock to him. Educated at Oxford, he came from a refined background and from a strictly Anglican persuasion, with its sense of order and morality. In his North Somerset parish, this vicar, smartly dressed in stocks and pantaloons, was introduced to drunkenness, immorality, lack of discipline and lack of religion, or worse still Methodism and Roman Catholicism.

It was quite a culture shock for the nervous, irritable and insecure gentleman who suffered private sorrow with the death of his wife, followed by the loss of his favourite daughter, leaving him with two sons and a daughter. At Camerton he was exposed to hard-living miners, to drunks at the Red Post Inn, to women of ill-repute. And he took every opportunity, whilst being charitable to them with one hand, to lecture them on their sinning with the other. It was his constant 'holier than thou' attitude which caused him to be so unpopular amongst his flock. He became fixated with the opinion that Camerton men were far more corrupt those elsewhere, and that the majority of his parishioners were sordid and disgusting.

When Mrs Gooch, whose miserable life had driven her to drink and ultimately madness, fell into a fire and later died from the burns, Skinner berated the Poor Law officials for having driven her to such depths through their meagreness. Then he blamed the magistrates who had reduced the amount paid to the Poor Law officials, and the alehouse which sold her the alcohol, and the Methodists for having failed to stop her drinking.

The landlord of the Red Post Inn received a volley of flack for allowing Farmer Lippeat to get so drunk that he fell into a quarry on the way home, killing himself in the process. In July 1809, he wrote:

William Britain of Cridlingcot died of consumption, brought on in a great measure by excessive drinking ...He declared solemnly to me that the Red Post public house had been his ruin; that frequently on Sunday he left his home with the intention of going to Camerton church, but as he crossed Whitebrooks Lane in his way thither something used to draw him away as it were, contrary to his better resolutions, and take him up the hill, where there was always a number of people assembled drinking all the Sunday morning.

Poor Mr Britain, clearly drawn away from the church to the inn by a stronger magnet.

Skinner criticised Mr and Mrs Hicks, the parish overseers, for allowing an invalid pauper to lie dying for ten days, being eaten alive by maggots. At the same time, he doled out charity in the form of cash, soup and medicine to the needy, and never understood how his parishioners could be so ungrateful towards him. And they were pretty vindictive in the retaliation. A man called Lowe, who had been criticised by Skinner, decided to take two pot shots with a gun at Skinner's dog whilst it roamed the rectory gardens. Farmers refused to pay their tithes. Even his sons refused to help him. He became obsessed, convinced that the whole community was plotting against him. Mrs Jarrett's peacocks would sit under his window and scream all night – and he was convinced that they picked on him deliberately. When one of his children accidentally broke a chair, he argued that all three children had plotted to annoy him, and he sent them away to Bath. During his church services, villagers would deliberately heckle him during the sermon.

A right holy pile up

He no doubt felt that the Bishop of Bath and Wells had also singled him out when he was involved in a most unfortunate accident. Travelling with horse and light carriage to Axbridge in 1830, Skinner joined a group of gypsies who were travelling with a line of donkeys to the fore. Joining on at the rear, he heard the sound of carriage wheels rapidly approaching from behind. It was raining and as he rode he held an umbrella aloft, no doubt obscuring his view of the approaching carriage, but he moved to one side of the road to give the advancing carriage room to pass. Unfortunately the carriage swerved the same way to avoid the donkeys and the two collided. Skinner shot forward, landing heavily in the middle of the road, momentarily stunned. Anger welled up inside him as he came to terms with his humiliation – and then realised the offending driver was none other than the Bishop of Bath and Wells. Rector and bishop completed the journey in the bishop's carriage whilst the gypsies kindly repaired Skinner's smaller rig before sending it on to him.

Skinner's solution to his persecution was to hide himself in books and, in particular, his theory that the Roman town of Camalodunum was not Colchester, as all other experts agreed, but Camerton. He would lock himself away for days at a time reading learned material, seeking any shred of evidence which might suggest his theory was correct. He wrote copiously and what started as a learned treatise gradually became a personal diary. In total he wrote 98 volumes of manuscripts and kept himself safely locked away from his flock in so doing.

10

The Vicars' Legacies

The bells

Many vicars and priests are well remembered for their deeds whilst serving their parish, indeed even immortalised through their legacies, leaving bell towers, schools, even a lighthouse! Moorlinch and Stawell are sister parishes, each boasting a bell tower thanks to the Lord Abbot, but only one has the bells. These two parishes were in dispute along with Chilton Polden, Catcott, Edington, Greinton and Sutton Mallet, all being villages on one side or the other of the Polden Hill ridge. The dispute was over who would get a set of church bells. The Lord Abbot of Glastonbury, who could only fund one set of bells, was keen to be seen to be fair and deemed that it would be appropriate that the bells should go to the church most likely to use them the most frequently. And so he made it a competition, the first parish to complete three christenings and three funerals would be the winners.

Stawell got off to a flying start with three christenings and two funerals in next to no time. They were so far out in the lead that their success was a foregone conclusion and so, in readiness for the bells, they enthusiastically commenced work on the bell tower. Meanwhile, Moorlinch had a christening and a funeral. As Stawell's bell tower progressed, Moorlinch had another funeral and a couple more christenings. Stawell began to panic. Had they jumped the gun? They desperately needed just one more funeral but the older members of the community stubbornly refused to die and Moorlinch pipped them to the post and installed their set of bells. Poor old Stawell capped off their rather shorter than average bell tower, started and finished prematurely.

Penance

Stogumber church in West Somerset was another to benefit from the goodwill of the Church's hierarchy. Cardinal Beaufort loved to hunt in Somerset and even had his own hunting lodge at Halsway Manor, near Bicknoller. One of his claims to fame was that he was involved in the execution of Joan of Arc and allegedly was one of those shouting 'Into the fire with the witch', even pushing her into the courtyard where the stake and fire awaited her arrival. Later he declared 'I will go and pray to her ashes'. Years later he paid for the north aisle of Stogumber church to be built, apparently as a penance for spending so much time hunting in the parish – no mention though of his penance for his involvement in the execution of Joan of Arc.

In an unrelated incident but again beginning in the early fifteenth century, a North Cadbury rector was to be attacked by the church bells, and a long time after he died. John Feron died in 1407. On his tombstone the inscription recorded how he had 'builded this tower at his own expense'. The thanks he got was quite unexpected when 150 years later the bell tower unexpectedly dumped its load, the bell crashing onto the rector's tomb, splitting the inscribed tombstone asunder. Such gratitude!

A lighthouse, a hymn and a school

Whilst some vicars left behind church towers, others left their own community-serving legacies, such as the Reverend David Davies of Burnham-on-Sea who provided the town with a lighthouse. The stretch of coast along Bridgwater Bay is notorious for its shifting sandbanks and difficult navigation. This story dates back to around 1750 when an old fisherman lived with his wife quite close to Burnham church. On a particularly stormy night, his good lady was growing concerned for her husband's safety. He had been out to sea, it was well after dark and he had not yet returned. She lit a candle and placed it in the window of their seafront cottage in the hope that it would guide him home. It did and the story of his survival spread through the fishing community.

The grateful sailors of Burnham agreed to pay the fisherman's wife a small regular fee to ensure a lighted candle was always placed in her window to guide them safely to shore. Some years later, the arrangement became more formalised when the sexton of the nearby church took on the role, paying the fisherman's wife £5 as compensation for loss of earnings. The church tower at least offered a higher and more effective vantage point.

Then in 1800, along came the Reverend David Davies, the curate of Burnham, who took the matter further still and had Burnham's first lighthouse built. It is not to be confused with the two lighthouses which we see today. Instead we must visit the house on the Esplanade known as the 'Round Tower', distinctive with its castellated top. Davies had it built at four-storeys tall at his own expense, and he had it built purposely to serve as a lighthouse. This time it was the church sexton who received the compensation, £20. In 1832 Trinity House took over the safety of shipping and erected the high and low lighthouses as we see them today.

A legacy of a very different nature was left to us by the Reverend Augustus Toplady, the curate of Blagdon. During the 1760s, he was travelling through Burrington Combe and was caught in a bitter storm. The wind was high and the rain was driving relentlessly through the rock-hewn landscape of the gorge. A loud roar of thunder followed the violent flash of fork lightening. The gorge, with its 250 feet high towering sides, was not the safest place to be. Toplady dashed into a cave where he was glad to find shelter. He mused on such thoughts as 'storms of life', 'rock of faith' and 'rock of ages'. The poetic words of a hymn were beginning to form in his mind: *Rock of ages, cleft for me; let me hide myself in thee'*. As he looked down at the floor of the cave he spotted a playing card, the six of diamonds. He picked it up and on its back began to write the words which were by then flowing with ease, and the hymn we all know so well evolved as he jotted down his thoughts.

The Reverend Toplady and Burrington Combe

The cradle of free elementary education

Some hymns, such as *Rock of* Ages seem to go on forever, as do some schools, like Enmore's primary school founded by John Poole. The Reverend John Poole attended Blundell's School in Tiverton, as did R. D. Blackmore, author of *Lorna Doone*. John Poole was the nephew of Thomas Poole of Nether Stowey, the man responsible for Coleridge and Wordsworth coming to live in Somerset. But it is his nephew who is of interest to us here. At the age of twenty-six he was granted the living of Enmore by Lord Egremont, in other words he became the vicar of Enmore. Apart from being a vicar, builder and gardener, he was also a keen educationalist. The achievement for which he will be remembered is the foundation in 1810 of the Rector's Village School at Enmore, where at one time he was the only teacher.

He was a great believer that every scholar should in turn become a teacher, and many of his pupils did just that. What was significant about his school was that it was the first free primary school in the country, and so successful was it that Wordsworth made an appeal for the introduction of a system of State Education. The school soon became famous with visitors from home and abroad, all coming to marvel at the academic achievements of its pupils. The school survives today and remains one of the most respected primary schools in the county, justifying its claim to be 'the cradle of free elementary school education'. Not one to sit on his laurels, Poole opened another and similar school in nearby Nether Stowey in 1813, the first teacher and head mistress being former pupils at Enmore.

Harvest home and the Reverend George Denison

It is a Somerset vicar to whom we can give credit for the popular harvest homes which are celebrated with gusto in the village communities. From pagan times, the end of the harvesting season was celebrated with displays of fruit and flowers, with corn dollies adorning the proceedings as if to confirm the pagan pedigree. The Christian Church adopted these celebrations, taking them into the churches and chapels as harvest festivals. However, in the middle of the nineteenth century, there were some vicars who were concerned that they had not engaged the farmers themselves who remained somewhat remote from the Church. There was also competition between the Anglican and Roman Catholic faiths. The Reverend George Denison, for sixty-one-years the rector of East Brent, came up with the idea of the harvest home, a celebration in a tent with plenty of food and drink, with music and dancing, with speeches and prayers of gratitude for the harvest. The tent would be decorated with flowers and garlands, corn dollies and sheaves of corn, and those gathered would sing aloud 'We plough the fields and scatter the good seed on the land'. It brought the community together and engaged those who were normally less than approachable where Church affairs were concerned.

Originally the convention was that the harvest home was celebrated once the last head of corn had been cut and the haywain was on its way back to the farm. The team of horses would be decorated with flowers and the lads and lasses would walk behind singing harvest songs. The last heads of corn would be used to create a corn dolly and the gathered throng would return to the farm house. It was from this practice that the harvest home developed but today they are huge events and need a great deal of planning. The timing is no longer dependent on the last of the corn being gathered in, but on the available dates for marquees and the live entertainment.

The rector and the blind fiddler

Thurloxton was well blessed when they received the Reverend William Boone as their vicar. He was a man of great passion and tremendous courage, courage which served him well when he served as a naval chaplain with Lord Nelson. He was one of two particular characters on board Nelson's ship at the Battle of Copenhagen in 1801. It was a battle before which Nelson declared 'It is warm work; and the day may be the last to any of us at a moment. But mark you! I would not be elsewhere for thousands.'

He had anticipated the conflict well. It was indeed warm work, and hundreds were killed or severely wounded. Our two key characters on board were the future vicar of Thurloxton and a wooden-legged fiddler. Each in their own way worked to maintain the high morale on board the fighting ship, one with words of comfort and the other with a merry tune. They were well familiar with each other having served in earlier times at the Battle of Cape St Vincent where the chaplain had stared death in the face, only to be saved by the fiddler. In saving the chaplain's life, the fiddler had lost his leg and henceforth sported a wooden one. Then at the Battle of Copenhagen, history repeated itself and this time the fiddler lost his sight whilst saving the chaplain's life. It was these actions which understandably bonded the two men so closely together.

On their retirement from naval service, the two men went their separate ways. The chaplain took up his post as the vicar of Thurloxton. There he became a well respected and indeed much loved member of the community, famous for his hospitality and kindness to those less fortunate than himself. It was not unusual therefore to find ill-kempt vagrants within his walls whilst they recovered from their trials.

On a bitterly-cold night, a bedraggled old man came to his door, half dead and in need of shelter. The vicar noticed the violin case the man carried as one of his few possessions. Nor could he fail to notice the presence of his wooden leg. Could this be the old blind fiddler to whom he owed so much, who had followed him loyally from ship to ship until they parted company with the Navy? Indeed the man appeared to be quite blind.

Too weak to talk, the man confirmed his identity by nodding his head. It was a full month before he was able to speak, and then only to ask for his fiddle. Taking up his fiddle for one final performance, he held it to his chin and played with such emotion as to bring the vicar close to tears, as if the man's soul were journeying to paradise with each note that he played. He passed the violin back to the rector and drifted into eternal rest. As a last act of loyalty, the vicar laid his friend to rest in the village churchyard.

The son of a preacher man

Whilst some vicars were to leave us notable legacies, like church towers and lighthouses, for others they left us their offspring who were to leave us legacies such as the fork, *Lorna Doone* and an Admiral or two. The Reverend Samuel Hood, the vicar of Butleigh, left the nation with two admirable sons, both of whom followed careers at sea. Samuel (Junior) was born in 1724, entered the navy as a midshipman at the age of sixteen and became a rear admiral, later to become Viscount Hood. Alexander, his junior by two years, became Commander of the Channel Fleet and was later created as Lord Bridport.

Whilst the Reverend Samuel Hood's sons travelled far and wide by sea, the son of George Coryate, the rector of Odcombe, travelled almost as extensively by foot. Thomas Coryate was born in the rectory in 1577.

Educated at Oxford, he failed his exams but found alternative employment as court jester to James l. In 1608, aged thirty-one, he set off on a 2000 mile hike around Europe, entirely on foot, and using the same pair of shoes throughout. On his return he literally hung up his shoes so that everyone could see that his walking days were over. He then spent his time writing about his exploits and adventures on his tour. He was an extremely intelligent man, very quick thinking. On one occasion he came upon a band of robbers. Aware that they would hold him up and take all he had, perhaps murdering him in the process, he quickly took off his hat, placed it on the ground before them and begged for alms – which they gave him and wished him well.

He also left a legacy which we all use today. In his days of travel, food was often delivered to the table in a communal bowl. All the diners would just dip their hands into the bowl, taking whatever they wished. It was very unhygienic, especially in the days of plague and with dysentery being a common occurrence. It was Thomas Coryate who introduced the table fork.

Four years after he hung up his walking boots, he got itchy feet once more and headed for the Middle East. It was a trip from which he was not to return, dying from dysentery in Surat.

And a daughter who travelled even further

The Reverend Doctor John Trevor was the rector of Otterhampton near Bridgwater. With two daughters already, in 1769 his wife gave birth to twin girls, Elizabeth and Frances. Shortly after, his wife died and then, aged seven, Elizabeth died. The vicar re-married, this time to Harriet Smith, a Bridgwater lady and four sons were born from that partnership. When Frances was seventeen, the family moved to Ostend, where her father was the chaplain to the English community. Whilst there, on the quayside one morning, a ship sailed in with a handsome captain, the twenty-six-year-old Captain Charles Barkley. The two met, fell in love and within weeks were married.

When Captain Barkley set sail, Frances's father stood on the quayside to wave goodbye to his daughter. She had joined her husband's ship and was on her way to the coast of British Columbia, surviving the storms around Cape Horn and the hostile natives of Hawaii. She was the first European woman to set foot on Hawaii, Alaska and British Columbia. Having traded with the North American Indians for sea otter pelts, they sailed with a full cargo to China. En route they were captured by Vietnamese pirates. Taken ashore as prisoners, the Vietnamese women were fascinated by the large pins which held Frances's hair up in a bun. Extracting the pins as decorative items, Frances's hair, free from restraint, cascaded down her back. Bright-shining red, it glowed in the sun and the native women were convinced that she must be a goddess – and they were all set free.

This was just one of many adventures which she experienced on a journey which made her the first woman, other than a French stowaway disguised as a man, to have circumnavigated the world. Within two years, she had repeated the trip and was certainly the first woman to sail around the world twice. What a contrast for this convent educated girl whose life until then had been confined to the graces of a Somerset vicar's refined residence.

Sidney Smith

Whilst some left us churches, and others left us hymns, or memorable sons and daughters, Sydney Smith left us the lasting legacy of his wit and humour. Combe Florey, during the years 1820 to 1831, was the home of this eccentric clergyman, writer and infamous wit. He was born in 1771, ordained into the Church of England in 1794 and then lived in Edinburgh, London and Yorkshire before moving to Somerset to serve the parish of Combe Florey. He was perhaps more at home in the cities for he described his move to the Somerset countryside as 'a kind of healthy grave' but having settled in, he announced that he was extremely pleased with Combe Florey. He was a great practical joker and in trying to convince his city friends of the mild climate in Somerset, tied oranges to his fruit trees. When one visitor declared that, whilst the climate was demonstrably warmer, the grounds of his house would look all the grander with the presence of some wild Red Deer, Smith came up with a solution. He attached sets of antlers to his bemused donkeys.

His eccentric style, instantaneous wit and immediate ability to break the ice with complete strangers completely threw the locals who were more accustomed to their vicars being of a serious, even dour nature. But he soon won their hearts and minds and not only became vicar but doctor, for he had trained originally in medicine, and was a much respected magistrate. He was a lover of truth and justice and had a way with words for which he became famous. He used that word power in a most practical way, defending the underdog and the oppressed. He also had little time for those in high places who took advantage of their positions.

He was a keen advocate of parliamentary reform and of Catholic emancipation. Perhaps his failure to rise through the ranks resulted from the occasional political comments he made, such as when he made a speech at Taunton in October 1831 when he compared the House of Lords with Mrs Partington of Sidmouth who set out with mop and buckets to hold back an Atlantic storm. It was expected that when the Whigs regained Parliament, he would get his promotion – but it was not to be.

As a preacher, he could fill a church to overflowing through the use of simple words and by treating his congregation and himself as on the same level. He never took his wit into the pulpit with him, he treated his pastoral duties seriously, but he seldom missed an opportunity when off duty. In describing Lord Macaulay, who was noted for the excessive use of words where a few could have captured the essence, Smith said with a clever balance of sarcasm and diplomacy 'There were gorgeous flashes of silence that made his conversation perfectly delightful.' In voicing his opinion on the report that a young man was to marry a widow twice his age and three times his size, he said:

Going to marry her? Impossible! You mean a part of her; he could not marry her all himself. It would be a case, not of bigamy but trigamy; there is enough of her to furnish wives for the whole parish. One man marry her! - it is monstrous! You might people a colony with her; or give an assembly with her; or perhaps take your morning's walk round her, always provided there were frequent resting places, and you were in rude health. I once was rash enough to try walking round her before breakfast, but only got half way and gave it up exhausted. Or you might read the Riot Act and disperse her; in short, you might do anything but marry her!

When a fellow clergyman wrote to him, pompously dating the letter with a reference to the saint's day on which it fell, rather than the conventional form for presenting the date, Smith replied by dating his letter as 'Washing Day'. When an uninvited and unwanted lady visited him wearing a crimson gown, he commented that it was exactly the colour of his preaching cushion and then waxed lyrical about the fabric and, approaching the lady with hands outstretched, declared 'I can hardly keep my hands off it. I shall be preaching on you, I fear.' The lady summoned her carriage and left as fast as was humanly possible. When visited by another lady who was complaining of the oppressive heat, he replied 'Heat! It was dreadful. I found I could do nothing for it but take off my flesh and sit in my bones.' When the lady asked, somewhat shocked, how he could do that, he replied 'Come and see me next time ma'am – nothing more easy!' with which she likewise beat a hasty retreat.

Sydney Smith enjoyed his food and drink but was somewhat overweight. Advised by his doctor that he should take regular walks on an empty stomach, he asked the doctor whose stomach he should walk on. Even on his death bed, he joked with his nurse. She was looking for a bottle of medication but could only find a bottle of ink in the place where the medicine should have been. Smith laughed as he contemplated the prospect that perhaps his last dose had been ink. When asked by the nurse what she should do he replied 'Bring me all the blotting paper there is in the house.'

Sydney Smith's witty answer to the old parish clerk.
From: The Wits and Beaux of Society
by Grace Wharton and Philip Wharton, 1861

11

Tales of the Unexpected

Naked ambitions

The church at Isle Brewers can boast a rather unusual association with a most extrovert character. It was rebuilt in 1861 at the expense of Dr Joseph Wolff. Born in Bavaria, he was the son of a Jewish rabbi and became a Christian. Amongst his many claims to fame is the fact that he was the first modern Christian missionary to preach to the Jews in Jerusalem. He also travelled extensively in eastern parts searching for the Lost Tribes of Israel. After one hike of 600 miles, he arrived naked and penniless in Kabul in Afghanistan. And he was not the first Somerset pilgrim to arrive naked in the Middle East. In mediaeval times, a Bridgwater woman from Orlieu Street travelled on a pilgrimage to Palestine, where she hung upside-down and naked for two days, as a self-inflicted penance, before travelling on to Avignon.

Muchelney's monk and the abandoned nun

During the fifteenth-century, down in Cornwall, the fifteenth-year-old son of a farmer fell in love with a girl called Drusilla. The feelings were mutual and both of them knew that it was in each other's company that they wanted to spend the rest of their lives. Matthew's father was a stubborn man and had already made up his mind that his son would marry the daughter of one of his best friends. Matthew knew that he could only ever marry Drusilla but felt unable to defy his father in such a way. His solution was to remove himself from the problem by dedicating himself to the Church and becoming a monk.

All Drusilla knew was that Matthew had gone far away. Heartbroken, and feeling betrayed, she entered a convent and locked herself away from the cruel world outside.

The years passed and Matthew rose to become a prior and was based at Muchelney Abbey. In his moments of contemplation, sitting on the banks of the River Parrett, watching herons fly by, his thoughts would drift back to his youth and his lost love. He found that as the days passed, the thoughts of his lost love visited him with increasing frequency, and it troubled him, wandering why he should become increasingly disturbed rather than time acting as a healer.

He was asked to visit the nearby nunnery to take a service there and to receive confessions. He was only too pleased to have something to do which perhaps would distract his thoughts away from his Drusilla. At the nunnery, he took the service and then, one by one, he took the confessions of the nuns until one particular nun unsettled him and he called an abrupt halt to the proceedings. She had confessed that her thoughts were being continually distracted by recollections of her lost love. Even during her prayers, her thoughts would return to Matthew, the man who had walked out of her life. Matthew asked for her name and she replied 'Drusilla'. Matthew was dumbstruck, halted the proceedings and prepared to leave.

He was visibly unsettled as he left the confessional. As he turned to go, Drusilla caught a glimpse of his face and realised that the man to whom she had delivered her confession was the very same man that was at the root of her unease. Matthew sought and was granted permission to be excused from taking confessions at the nunnery. Nonetheless for the next year he could not eradicate thoughts of Drusilla from his mind. At the end of that year, he was asked to once more take confession at the nunnery and, no one else being available, he was not in a position to refuse.

As each nun in turn entered the confessional, he wandered if the next would be Drusilla – but the queue ended and she had not appeared. As he was preparing to leave, the Mother Superior asked him to deliver the Last Sacrament to a nun who was dying. She explained how the nun had been taken ill a year before, for no apparent reason, as if she had lost the will to live. Now, in a dreadfully weakened state, it was felt she possibly would not last the night. Matthew entered the nun's cell and recognised the thin form of Drusilla, a shadow of her former self. In her weakened state, she looked up, recognised him and asked him to forgive her, which of course he did. He delivered the Last Sacrament and told her that he loved her still. Struggling to lift herself, and struggling to be heard, she declared that she too still loved him – with which she sank back and breathed her last. As Matthew closed her eyelids, a tear rolled down her cheek.

She was buried by the monks from Muchelney. Years later Matthew too went to meet his maker. He was buried with his bible, within the front cover of which was inscribed 'I love you, Drusilla, Drusilla my love.'

The Reverend Byam, the Turk, a ghost and the Civil War

The Exmoor village of Luccombe lies at the base of Dunkery Hill. Its one-time vicar in the sixteenth century was the Reverend Byam, who was succeeded in 1612 by his son, the Reverend Dr Henry Byam. Educated at Oxford, he took on his father's parish and within two years had also adopted nearby Selworthy. His life whilst serving the Church was full of incidents and his fame spread well beyond the boundaries of Exmoor.

Perhaps the first notable incident came in 1620 when he converted a Muslim to Christianity. It was the practice of pirates from North Africa to capture people to sell into slavery. Occasionally they would raid the West Country coast and capture ships and their sailors. In that way, a young Minehead sailor had ended up as a captive of the pirates and was being held in Algiers. Life as a slave was diabolical; hours of slave labour, floggings, poor food and the constant threat that if you fell ill or collapsed on the job, death was inescapable. No one would feed a slave who couldn't pay his way in labour.

There was however, one possible escape route and that was to 'Turn Turk', which was the western expression for accepting the Muslim faith. The Algerian pirates would not enslave a Muslim. Christians were their target. And so the young Minehead sailor adopted Islam. The stringent conditions previously imposed on him were then relaxed and he was able to escape and make his way back to Minehead.

Once returned to the bosom of his family, his story unfolded and it was realised that he had renounced Christianity and become a Muslim. He was an Infidel! And it was for this problem that our vicar from Luccombe was called in. It was his role to arrange a re-admission to the Christian faith. The young sailor stood before the congregation at St Michael's church in his Muslim dress. As the service progressed, he cast off his clothes and, naked, was welcomed back into the Christian Church.

The Reverend Byam was called back to Minehead many years later, once again to carry out a task too complicated for others to perform. Old Mother Leakey had been the popular mother of a Minehead trader, well loved by all during her lifetime, but detested after her death in 1634. Her ghost came back to haunt the town and she terrorised the townsfolk, including the local doctor who she would chase across the fields, kicking his backside as she chased him. She then turned to sinking ships and it was at this stage that the local vicar called for the Reverend Byam to assist in exorcising her ghost.

Byam, however, was not convinced by the stories he was told and referred the matter to the bishop, who set up an enquiry. The conclusion of the investigation was that the stories held no water and if the local vicar could stay sober for long enough, then perhaps he could re-establish contact with reality!

Whether Old Mother Leakey then disappeared, or whether the Minehead vicar sobered up, we will never know. But we do know that Mother Leakey was never seen again.

In later years, Byam's life was to be plagued with tragedy. He was a staunch Royalist and at the beginning of the Civil War in 1642, he raised a troop of cavalry in support of Charles 1. Four of his sons became captains, and all died fighting for the cause. In 1645, when Cromwell's forces were sweeping down through the West Country, Byam's wife and daughter drowned in the Bristol Channel during their attempt to escape to safety. The Reverend Byam meanwhile had escaped to the Scilly Isles with the Royalist forces, and later to Jersey. He lived there for a while before returning to Somerset where he lived in enforced obscurity.

When Charles 11 came to the throne, our vicar returned to Luccombe albeit his lands had all been confiscated by Cromwell. Nonetheless, Charles 11 repaid Byam's loyalty to the royal family by appointing him to the position of Canon of Exeter and Prebendary of Wells. He died in 1669 and is buried in Luccombe church where his tomb occupies a commanding position.

The disappearing Reverend Benjamin Speke

There is a tendency to think that stress is a modern phenomenon, a twentieth century invention. But as far back as 1868 we can find a tale of a Somerset vicar who decided that he had had enough and would simply disappear.

For eleven years the Reverend Benjamin Speke had been the rector at Dowlish Wake, perhaps now best known for 'Perry's Cider Mill'. The Speke family's West Country pedigree dated back to the twelfth century and Benjamin's family inherited the manor of Dowlish Wake. The family could also boast a succession of rectors in the area and it was in 1857 that Benjamin accepted the position of rector to the village.

Eleven years into his role, he travelled to London to preside at a friend's wedding. It was January 1868. His brother-in-law was expecting him at this London home. Without announcing himself, Benjamin dropped off his luggage at the house, went to a hat shop in

Pimlico, and then disappeared without trace.

His family were devastated. Benjamin was the fourth and youngest son of the family. His eldest brother William was married but with no children. His next brother was Captain John Hanning Speke, famous explorer and discoverer of the source of the Nile. He had died, unmarried, as the result of a shooting accident. The third son, Edward, had been killed in India during the Great Indian Mutiny. Benjamin was the family's last chance of providing a male heir.

A London detective was employed and a £100 reward offered for information. Every London newspaper carried an advertisement describing thirty-seven-year-old Benjamin's appearance and making reference to the reward. The sole result was the discovery of his newly purchased hat in Birdcage Walk. The reward was increased to £500.

The newspapers were full of speculation; had he been abducted? Murdered? Rumours spread like wildfire: his body had been found in an attic; he had been discovered in a German lunatic asylum; he was serving as a missionary in North Africa. All of this speculation turned out to be inaccurate.

At the end of February, a Cornish police officer in Padstow was tracking down an absconded bankrupt and arrested a man dressed as a bullock driver who fitted the description. On checking the contents of the man's pockets, he was found to have £200 in notes and gold, a small fortune which did not fit with the garb of a bullock driver. The officer considered that in all probability he had arrested a robber, possibly even a murderer. The man claimed that he was Benjamin Speke and related how he had travelled from London via Basingstoke and Winchester, partly walking and partly working his way down to Cornwall.

Asked why he had disappeared, he explained that he felt unwanted by his family, perhaps the result of living in the shadow of his more illustrious brothers. Hence he had deliberately disappeared, with the eventual intention of travelling to America to start a new life, preaching the gospel. The real cause, however, was his family's strong objection to his intended marriage to his cousin. They were deeply in love, more so than the family could ever have realised.

He was sent to France for a period of rest. Meanwhile, the £500 was sent to the Cornwall Constabulary, destined for Sgt. Soady, who had discovered, arrested and identified Benjamin Speke. Unfortunately it got no further than the Deputy Chief Constable and his Superintendent, much to the anger of the press. Soady received nothing.

In 1869, the Reverend Benjamin Speke returned to Dowlish Wake and married his cousin, Caroline Fuller, and they produced the much sought after heirs, seven sons and a daughter. Benjamin's wife died in the twelfth year of their marriage. The following day the Reverend Benjamin Speke committed suicide, drowning himself in a deep tank at Wake Hill House. They were buried together in Dowlish Wake churchyard having provided one of Somerset's most tragic true-life love stories.

Bibliography

Bush, Robin (1997), *Somerset Bedtime Book*; Wimborne, Dovecote Press

Bush, Robin (1990), *Somerset Stories*; Wimborne, Dovecote Press

Dunning, Robert (Ed) (1976), *Christianity in Somerset*; Taunton, Somerset County Council

Evans, Roger (1995), *Bridgwater with and without the 'e'*; Bridgwater, Roger Evans

Lawrence, Berta (1984), *Exmoor Villages*; Dulverton, The Exmoor Press

Holt, Alan (1992), *Folklore of Somerset*; Stroud, Alan Sutton Publishing Ltd

Holt, Alan (1984), *West Somerset Romantic Routes and Mysterious Byways*; Cheddar, Charled Skilton Ltd

Legg, Philippa and Binding, Hilary (1986), *Somerset Cider – The Complete Story*; Tiverton, Somerset Books

Mander, Charles (1976), *The Reverend Prince and his Abode of Love*; Wakefield, EP Publishing

Norris, Sally (1989), *Tales of Old Somerset*; Newbury, Countryside Books

Quaife, G. R. (1979), *Wanton Wenches and Wayward Wives*; London, Croom Helm Ltd

Powys, Llewelyn (1986), *Scenes from Somerset Childhood*; Bristol, Recliffe Press

Poyntz-Wright, Peter (1983), *The Rural Bench Ends of Somerset*; Amersham, Avebury Publishing

Stubbs, Philip (1583), *The Anatomie of Abuses*; London, R. Jones

Sweet, Jack W. (1999), *Shocking Somerset Stories*; Tiverton, Somerset Books

Tongue, R. L. (1965), *Somerset Folklore*; Folklore Society

Underdown, David (1985), *Revel, Riot and Rebellion*; Oxford, OUP

Underwood, Peter (1985), *Ghosts of Somerset*; Bodmin, Bossiney Books

Wharton, Grace and Philip (1861), *The Wits and Beaux of Society*; New York, Harper